Political
Participation
in the
United States

Political Participation in the United States

SECOND EDITION

(mary margaret)

M. Margaret Conway

University of Florida

PRESS

A Division of Congressional Quarterly Inc.

Washington, D.C.

Library of Congress Cataloging-in-Publication Data

Conway, M. Margaret (Mary Margaret), 1935–
   Political participation in the United States / M. Margaret Conway.
—2nd ed.
      p.   cm.
   Includes bibliographical references and index.
ISBN 0-87187-539-X
   1. Political participation—United States.   2. Political
participation—United States—History.   I. Title.
JK1764.C548   1990
323'.042'0973—dc20   90-47357
                                                               CIP

Contents

Tables

Preface

In an era of astounding developments in many other political systems brought about through significant changes in the forms and levels of their citizens' political participation, the United States continues to have low levels of citizen participation. Those patterns are reported and analyzed in this book. Scholars continue to try to solve the various puzzles presented by these low levels of participation in American politics, and the results of their efforts are also reported in this book.

Political scientists differ in their views of the role of political participation in a democracy, but all are concerned with its consequences for the stability and effectiveness of democratic systems of government. This book examines the nature and extent of political participation in the United States, and presents various explanations for its causes. The consequences of patterns of political participation for citizens themselves and for public policy are also examined.

Historical trends in political participation are presented in Chapter 1. Chapter 2 looks at the effects of selected life-experience variables on political participation, including those associated with differences in age, education, gender, ethnicity, race, region, and employment.

Patterns of political participation also vary with the attitudes, beliefs, and values held by citizens. Chapter 3 examines trends over time in psychological orientations, such as political trust, efficacy, interest in politics, and concern with the outcome of elections, as well as the relationships between patterns of psychological orientations and various forms of political participation.

Many aspects of the political system affect patterns of political participation. These include the nature of the party system; political movements, such as the civil rights, women's, and anti-

Vietnam War movements; and the mass media's coverage of politics. These are discussed in Chapter 4.

The legal right to participate effectively in politics is taken for granted by most Americans, but both our recent history and those of many other nations demonstrate that access to effective participation in the political system can be limited or shaped by a number of legal, and sometimes illegal, means. Legal means include election laws and election administration procedures. The effects of the legal structure on suffrage in America are discussed in Chapter 5.

The question can be raised, When there are so many citizens eligible to participate, is participation by any one citizen rational? How can one person have any impact on the political system and its policy outputs? That issue is addressed in Chapter 6.

In Chapter 7, all the different factors discussed separately in the previous chapters—who participates, in what way, and to what effect—are examined as they relate to one another. Finally, Chapter 8 considers whether political participation has an instrumental effect or is merely symbolic action that provides support and legitimation to the structures of government, particular political leaders, and the political system as a whole.

Preparation of the second edition has benefited from the valuable suggestions of Paul Abramson of Michigan State University and Denise Baer of the University of Akron. Research assistance was provided by Glenn Silver and Mari Thomas. Computer support for research on political participation was provided by the Computer Science Center, University of Maryland, and the computer facilities of the University of Florida.

Some of the data used in this book were made available by the Inter-University Consortium for Political and Social Research. The data for the American National Election Studies were collected by the Center for Political Studies, Institute for Social Research, University of Michigan, under grants funded by the National Science Foundation. Neither the original collectors of the data nor the consortium bears any responsibility for the analyses or interpretations presented here.

My appreciation also goes to Joanne Daniels, former CQ Press director, to Margaret Benjaminson, Ann O'Malley, and Nancy Lammers of CQ Press, and to Lys Ann Shore, who edited the manuscript for this edition.

Political
Participation
in the
United States

Chapter 1

Introduction

Viewing the United States in 1831, Frenchman Alexis de Tocqueville saw politics as the American passion. "The political activity that pervades the United States must be seen in order to be understood. No sooner do you set foot on American ground than you are stunned by a kind of tumult."[1] Is that widespread passion for politics still present in our country? One example indicates the nature of the answer. In 1990, Texas held a primary election for governor, with three well-known candidates vying for the Democratic nomination and several widely recognized candidates contesting the Republican primary; nominations for many other offices were being made at the same time. The gubernatorial candidates alone spent a record $28 million on the primary contests, which featured numerous accusations and countercharges, rancorous formal debates, and extensive news coverage. Yet only three out of ten eligible Texans bothered to vote. Why was turnout so low? In postelection interviews, journalists sought to answer that question. Suggested answers elicited by the reporters from the nonvoting public ranged from "cynicism to ignorance to contentment to laziness."[2]

While primary turnout is always lower than general election participation, the 1990 Texas primary illustrates a more general pattern. Voting participation in presidential elections has declined significantly over the past three decades, and in 1988, electoral turnout for the presidential election was the lowest it has been since 1924.

How can nonvoting be explained? Do people who do not vote

engage in other forms of political participation? Who engages in political action, and how can patterns of political participation be explained? This book addresses those and many other questions about the causes, patterns, and consequences of political participation.

What is the role of citizen participation in a democracy? Traditional democratic theory assumes that citizens in a democratic state are interested in and participate in politics, are knowledgeable about the process of government and the proposed alternative solutions to public problems, and vote in accord with a set of values or principles.[3] Studies of the electorate in democratic nations, however, indicate that these assumptions are unrealistic. For example, in the United States, many citizens are uninterested in public affairs. Participation rates are low. Only a small proportion of the electorate has much knowledge about the structure and functions of government, and the mass public is often unaware of even major policy problems being considered by federal, state, or local governments. Many voters cast their votes on the basis of group attachments or the personal characteristics of candidates and lack knowledge of the candidates' stands even on issues that are important to them.[4]

Revisionists of classical democratic theory argue that low levels of political participation and interest actually contribute to governmental stability.[5] Furthermore, some revisionists contend that because many people are not interested in most issues before the government, it is easier for those who are concerned to work out compromises on divisive issues. Low levels of political interest and participation in public affairs are interpreted as reflecting satisfaction with the operating processes and policy outputs of the political system.[6]

Perhaps, then, the requirements for a stable democracy specified by classical democratic theory are not met. And yet stable democracies, such as the United States and Great Britain, do exist. Scholars have therefore suggested an alternative set of conditions. These conditions include: (1) social pluralism, (2) diverse and competing elites that are circulating and accessible, (3) a basic consensus at least among the elites on the rules of democratic competition, and (4) elections that provide regular opportunities for citizens to participate in the selection of public officials.[7]

Nevertheless, the belief that widespread popular participation is necessary for the effective functioning of a stable democracy continues to find support, partly because participation is viewed as maintaining open access to the system. If the system is open to participation, then those who want to participate can do so in the event that an issue arises which is sufficiently important to motivate their participation. This raises the question of the extent to which barriers to political participation exist. These barriers may be structural, such as voter registration laws and election administration procedures, or they may be psychological, created by political learning processes that instill in some segments of American society weak levels of the orientations that facilitate political participation.

The revisionist view of democratic theory implies that participation is instrumental. To what extent does popular participation, when it occurs, have an impact on public policy, and to what extent is the mass public's participation merely ritualistic? This question can be posed in another form: Under what conditions is political participation rational? A decision to participate would be rational if a citizen (1) has specific preferences for certain policy outcomes over others, (2) can rank outcomes in an order of preference, (3) has a set of rules by which he or she can link preferences to actions that will contribute to obtaining the desired outcomes, and (4) chooses those alternatives that can contribute to obtaining the preferred outcome.[8] This last requirement raises a particular problem. Suppose a citizen is only one of nine million people who are eligible to vote, and five million are expected to vote on election day: Is participation rational when the chance that one citizen's vote will have an impact on the outcome is extremely small?

The Meaning of Political Participation

The term *political participation* is being used here to mean those activities of citizens that attempt to influence the structure of government, the selection of government authorities, or the policies of government. These activities may be supportive of the existing policies, authorities, or structure, or they may seek to change any or all of these. This definition emphasizes active involvement that is instrumental or goal-oriented. However, political participation also includes passive kinds of involvement, such as attending ceremonial or supportive activities, or paying attention to what is happening in the government or in politics. Thus, following political campaigns through the mass media could be considered a passive form of political participation. Similarly, paying attention to the activities and policy decisions of a city council, state legislature, or federal agency could be classified as passive political participation.

A distinction can be made between *conventional* and *unconventional* political participation.[9] Conventional participation refers to those activities that are accepted as appropriate by the dominant political culture. Voting, seeking elective office, working for a candidate or a political party, writing a letter to a public official—these are examples of conventional forms of political behavior. Another form of conventional political participation is organizational—working with others to obtain a particular outcome. The full range of public policies can be the focus of such activities, and organized groups try to influence policy at all levels of government. Examples of organizational activity include advocacy of a nuclear weapons freeze, efforts to end pollution of rivers, or an attempt to prevent the closing of a local school.

Other forms of political participation are not accepted as appropriate by the dominant political culture, even though they may be legal. A march by students in a college town to protest the fact that boundary lines for city-council districts were redrawn to weaken their political power would be legal, but the local residents might regard it as inappropriate. Some forms of political participation are both unconventional and illegal. For example, during the Vietnam War, a small group of radicals planted a bomb in a classroom and laboratory building at the University of Wisconsin, killing one student, because they believed that some of the research conducted in the building contributed to the war effort. Political protest in this form goes beyond what is acceptable to Americans and violates the law as well. Unconventional political behavior can be viewed as a continuum, ranging from participating in peaceful protest marches to engaging in terrorist violence or civil war.

Another form of political participation is activity aimed at the repression of either conventional or unconventional political participation.[10] Repression is most frequently aimed at protest behavior. During the 1950s and 1960s, sit-ins and demonstrations in support of civil rights for black citizens who were being denied their legal rights occurred in many areas of the country. These were countered by activities, sometimes by private citizens and sometimes by law enforcement authorities, that tried to halt these protests, even when they took the form of peaceful, lawful demonstrations.

Measurement of the frequency with which citizens engage in different types of political activities presents a number of problems. Voting is the simplest form of activity to measure, but even that is not without problems. *Voter turnout* is the percentage of the voting-age population that actually voted. One way of measuring it is to add up the number of votes cast for a particular office, such as the presidency, and divide the total by the number of people of voting age. However, some citizens vote but cast invalid ballots; others vote for some offices but not for a presidential candidate. Furthermore, it is generally recognized that the census undercounts the population; and since a census is taken only once every ten years, the size of the population in the intervening years must be estimated. Despite these problems, the percentage of the voting-age population that voted is probably the best estimate of voter turnout available.

Another method of calculating voter turnout is to draw a representative sample of the voting-age population and interview it. The Bureau of the Census uses this method, with a sample of fifty thousand or more households. The person interviewed in each household is asked whether each voting-age person in the household voted. The Bureau of the Census estimates that, because interviewees overreport the frequency of voting, turnout measured in this way is 5 to 15 percent higher than the true figure.[11] Other estimates of voting turnout are derived from much smaller representative samples, ranging from fifteen hundred to thirty-five hundred people, drawn from the voting-age population by the University of Michigan's Center for Political Studies for in-depth research on the beliefs, attitudes, and political participation of the American electorate. These surveys are a major source of information about other forms of political participation as well.[12]

Problems also exist in measuring other forms of political participation. Our knowledge of citizens' engagement in forms of political action other than voting depends on responses to survey questions about various kinds of political activity. While national surveys in election years frequently ask about campaign-related activities, collection of information about other kinds of participation, such as holding membership in politically relevant organizations, contacting public officials, or engaging in political protest activities, occurs much less frequently.

Trends in Political Participation

One cause of the American Revolution was the widely held belief that those who are governed have a right to be represented in the governmental decision-making process. That view was expressed in the slogan, "No taxation without representation." The usual mechanism for providing representation is an election. However, in the England of that time, the right to vote was sharply limited.[13] In the American colonies, the right to participate in elections to the colonial legislatures was limited to adult males; and because of additional restrictions, such as "good character," property ownership, or payment of taxes, less than half even of the adult males were eligible to vote in colonial America.[14]

After the revolution, most of the members of the electoral college (which actually chooses the president of the United States) were elected by the state legislatures, but by 1832, they were elected by popular vote in all but one of the states. However, only 22 percent of the adult population participated in that year.[15] (Nonwhite citizens were not allowed to vote in most states, and women did not have the legal right to vote in any state.) Voter turnout increased gradually thereafter, reaching

TABLE I-I
Voter Registration and Turnout, 1966–1988

Year	Percent registered	Percent voting
1966	70.3	55.4
1968	74.3	67.8
1970	69.1	54.6
1972	72.3	63.0
1974	62.2	44.7
1976	66.7	59.2
1978	62.6	45.9
1980	66.9	59.2
1982	64.1	48.5
1984	68.3	59.9
1986	64.3	56.0
1988	66.6	57.4

SOURCES: U.S. Department of Commerce, Bureau of the Census, "Voter Participation in November, 1972," Population Characteristics, Series P-20, No. 244 (Washington: Government Printing Office, December 1972), tables A and B; "Voting and Registration in the Election of November 1988," Series P-20, No. 440 (Washington: Government Printing Office, October 1989), tables A and B.

37.6 percent of the adult population in the election of 1876. Turnout averaged 36.1 percent in the presidential elections held between 1876 and 1896, but it then began to decline. After the amendment to the federal Constitution granting women the right to vote went into effect in 1920, turnout increased to 42.5 percent. Turnout attained a post-World War II high in 1960, but declined from 1960 to 1980. In 1984, it increased slightly, with 59.9 percent of the voting-age population participating, but decreased again in 1988, to 57.4 percent.[16]

Table I-I compares voter turnouts in elections of presidents with turnouts in elections of members of the House of Representatives. Fewer people cast votes in the congressional elections than in the presidential elections held at the same time. An even smaller proportion of the voting-age population votes in the congressional elections held in the middle of the president's four-year term of office.

While politicians often interpret their electoral victories as a "mandate from the people," such claims should be viewed with

TABLE 1-2

Percent of People Reporting Participating in Election-Related Activities, 1952–1988

Form of activity	Election year																	
	1952	1956	1958	1960	1962	1964	1966	1968	1970	1972	1974	1976	1978	1980	1982	1984	1986	1988
Tried to persuade others	28	28	17	34	18	31	22	33	27	32	15	37	22	36	23	32	21	29
Attended political meetings	7	7	—	8	8	9	—	9	9	9	6	6	10	8	9	8	7	7
Worked for party or candidate	3	3	—	6	4	5	—	6	7	5	5	4	6	4	6	4	3	3
Wore button or put bumper sticker on car	—	16	—	21	10	17	—	15	9	14	5	8	9	7	8	9	7	9
Gave money to a party or candidate	4	10	—	12	9	11	8	9	—	10	8	16	13	16[a]	17	12[a]	10	8
Wrote letter to public official	—	—	—	—	—	17	—	20	27	27	—	28	—	—	—	—	—	—

SOURCES: Data for 1952–1978 from Warren E. Miller, Arthur H. Miller, and Edward J. Schneider, *American National Election Studies Data Sourcebook, 1952–1978* (Cambridge: Harvard University Press, 1980), 304–305, tables 5.1–5.6. Copyright © 1980 by the President and Fellows of Harvard College, used by permission. Data for 1980 from Warren E. Miller and the American National Election Studies, *American National Election Study, 1980* (Ann Arbor, Mich.: Inter-University Consortium for Political and Social Research, 1982), vol. 1, *Pre- and Post-Election Surveys*. Data for 1982, 1984, 1986, and 1988 from the American National Election Studies, Center for Political Studies, University of Michigan.

[a] Includes contributions to political action committees as well as to parties and candidates.

considerable skepticism. The winning candidate usually receives the vote of substantially less than 50 percent of the voting-age population. Since 1920, the presidential candidate who had the greatest popular vote was Lyndon Johnson, and he received the votes of only 37.8 percent of the voting-age population in 1964. The president with the lowest level of support during that period was Calvin Coolidge, who was elected by the votes of 23.7 percent of the voting-age population in 1924. He is closely followed by Harry Truman in 1948 (25.3 percent), Jimmy Carter in 1976 (27.2 percent), and Ronald Reagan in 1980 (27.3 percent).[17]

Survey research conducted since 1952 indicates that citizen participation in other forms of election-related activity is even less frequent than voting (see Table 1-2). The commonest of these other forms is trying to persuade others how to vote; since 1952, the proportion of the electorate reporting that they have engaged in that activity has ranged from 28 to 37 percent in presidential years and from 17 to 27 percent in midterm years. Substantially lower proportions report participating in other ways in political campaigns. Between 6 and 10 percent attended campaign rallies or political meetings. Wearing campaign buttons and displaying bumper stickers on cars, never higher than 21 percent, appears to have declined to less than 10 percent since the middle 1970s. That may be attributable to changes in federal campaign-finance laws, which at that time began requiring more rigorous accounting for campaign receipts and expenditures. The decline may also in part reflect the increased emphasis on radio and television advertising in political campaigns. The cost of buttons and bumper stickers and doubts about their effectiveness make campaign managers reluctant to expend limited funds on these types of advertising.

On the other hand, the proportion of people who contribute money to campaigns appears to have been higher from 1976 through 1982 than it was either before or since. This may reflect in part the increased use of targeted direct mail to solicit small political contributions from a larger proportion of the electorate, and the tax deductibility of small contributions during that period. As with other forms of campaign activity, a greater pro-

TABLE I-3
Levels of Political Interest, 1952–1988

	1952	1954	1956	1958	1960	1962	1964	1966	1968	1970	1972	1974	1976	1978	1980	1982	1984	1986	1988
Percent reporting general interest in politics:																			
most of the time	—	—	—	—	21	16	30	35	33	—	37	39	38	23	26	29	—	26	22
some of the time	—	—	—	—	42	43	42	30	31	—	36	36	31	34	35	35	—	35	37
Percent saying they were interested in the current campaign:																			
very much	37	—	30	27	38	36	38	30	39	34	32	—	37	22	30	26	35	23[b]	31
somewhat	34	—	40	33	37	38	37	40	40	43	41	—	42	45	44	44	45	44	46
not much	29	—	31	41	25	26	25	30	21	24	27	—	21	34	26	30	20	33	22
Percent saying they "care a good deal" which party wins the election[a]	67	—	63	53	65	—	66	—	65	65	60	57	57	43	56	—	66	64	61

SOURCE: American National Election Studies, Center for Political Studies, University of Michigan.

[a] Election of president in presidential years, of representative in midterm years.

[b] In 1986, the response categories were "care very much," "pretty much," "not very much," or "not at all." The percentage reported in the table is the sum of "very much" (18.4%) and "pretty much" (35.7%).

portion of citizens usually contributes money in presidential years than in midterm years.

A more passive form of political participation is for people to be interested in politics and to pay attention to political events. As Table 1-3 indicates, general political interest was higher from the mid-1960s to the mid-1970s than either before or since. The political environment of that period included the 1964 presidential campaign, which featured a contest between a conservative Republican, Barry Goldwater, and Lyndon Johnson, the first southerner nominated as a presidential candidate by either major political party since the Civil War. The candidates differed sharply on both foreign and domestic policy issues, with Goldwater advocating a greater American involvement in the war in Vietnam and a more confrontational policy toward Communist nations. By 1966, the United States had half a million military personnel in Vietnam, and the controversy over its involvement there generated great political interest. Another stimulus to political interest at the time was the set of events generally referred to as "Watergate," beginning in June 1972 with the arrest of four persons inside the Democratic party national headquarters in the Watergate office building and ending, after the initiation of impeachment proceedings in the House of Representatives, with the resignation of President Nixon on August 9, 1974.[18] Political interest continued at a high level until 1976 and then began to drop.

The proportion of people caring about who wins the election remained relatively stable in presidential elections until 1972, when it began to decline. This seems to correspond with the trend in voter turnout. Concern with the outcome of the election appears to have rebounded slightly with the 1984 and 1988 presidential elections. The fact that fewer people care who wins in congressional elections than in presidential elections also corresponds to the lower turnouts in midterm years.

Symbolic and Instrumental Participation

In the course of considering various forms of political participation, the question arises: To what extent is engaging in polit-

ical activity a symbolic act? Some types of political acts are easily
recognized as symbolic: saluting the flag, singing the national
anthem, reciting the pledge of allegiance. Performing symbolic
acts may serve to reduce citizens' resentments and doubts about
government institutions and policies, may reaffirm citizens' beliefs and attitudes that support governing institutions, and may
increase the likelihood that citizens will accept as legitimate the
political institutions and the policies they develop.[19] Of course,
citizens may also engage in symbolic acts that express their disapproval of government policies, leaders, and institutions.

Some forms of political participation generally regarded as
instrumental may also be symbolic. For example, voting in an
election can be a symbolic act. By voting, an individual expresses
support for the political system and may also give expression to
feelings of support for or opposition to a candidate, a party, or
certain policies. Some voters in effect keep a political "hit list"—
a list of candidates they want to vote against. Many politicians
believe that the vote against is more highly motivated than the
vote for a candidate; they therefore try very hard not to give
citizens any cause for placing them on a "hit list." Sometimes
voting may be used to express generalized disapproval, as when
the citizens of São Paulo, Brazil, elected a rhinoceros in the city
zoo to the city council in 1959.[20] In countries where citizens are
required to vote and have no choices to make, opposition can
be expressed by casting a blank ballot.[21] Obviously, such voting
behavior is also a symbolic act.

Political participation as instrumental action is performed
with a view to obtaining a specific personnel or policy outcome.
For example, some citizens may be quite aware of the policy
views and past legislative voting record of a congressional candidate on a particular issue, and when they decide how to vote
in the congressional election, they decide on the basis of that
issue. If these instrumental voters join with enough others who
vote the same way on the basis of the same or other policy issues,
they may have a decisive impact on the outcome of the election.
Thus, some forms of political participation can be both symbolic
and instrumental.

If political action is instrumental, then patterns of political participation will determine the distribution of the goods and services available through the political system. If political action is symbolic, we must consider how and why it is used both by those who seek to stimulate it and by those who engage in it, and what the consequences are.

NOTES

1. Alexis de Tocqueville, *Democracy in America*, ed. Phillips Bradley (New York: Vintage Books, 1957), 1:259.
2. David Maraniss, "Cynical or Lazy, Majority Didn't Vote," *Washington Post*, March 15, 1990, A3.
3. Bernard Berelson, "Democratic Theory and Public Opinion," *Public Opinion Quarterly* 16 (1952): 313–330; G. Bingham Powell, Jr., *Contemporary Democracies: Participation, Stability, and Violence* (Cambridge: Harvard University Press, 1982); and Carole Pateman, *Participation and Democratic Theory* (Cambridge: Cambridge University Press, 1970), chap. 1.
4. Bernard R. Berelson, Paul F. Lazarsfeld, and William N. McPhee, *Voting: A Study of Opinion Formation in a Presidential Campaign* (Chicago: University of Chicago Press, 1954), chap. 14; Lester W. Milbrath and M. L. Goel, *Political Participation*, 2d ed. (Chicago: Rand McNally, 1977); Angus Campbell, Philip E. Converse, Warren Miller, and Donald E. Stokes, *The American Voter* (New York: John Wiley, 1964); Ivor Crewe, "Political Participation," in *Democracy at the Polls*, ed. David Butler, Howard R. Penniman, and Austin Ranney (Washington, D.C.: American Enterprise Institute, 1981); Paul R. Abramson, John H. Aldrich, and David W. Rohde, *Change and Continuity in the 1984 Elections* (Washington, D.C.: CQ Press, 1986), 176–188; and *Change and Continuity in the 1988 Elections* (Washington, D.C.: CQ Press, 1990).
5. Seymour Martin Lipset, *Political Man: The Social Bases of Politics* (Baltimore: Johns Hopkins University Press, 1981); and Berelson, Lazarsfeld, and McPhee, *Voting*, chap. 14.
6. See, for example, Berelson, Lazarsfeld, and McPhee, *Voting*, chap. 14.
7. Roger W. Cobb and Charles D. Elder, *Participation in American Politics: The Dynamics of Agenda-Building*, 2d ed. (Baltimore: Johns Hopkins University Press, 1983). See also Berelson, Lazarsfeld, and McPhee, *Voting*, chap. 14; Gerald M. Pomper, with Susan S. Lederman, *Elections in America*, 2d ed. (New York: Longman, 1980), chaps. 2 and 10; and, for a comparative analysis of the role of political participation in contributing to political stability, Powell, *Contemporary Democracies*.
8. Norman Frohlich and Joe A. Oppenheimer, *Modern Political Economy* (Englewood Cliffs, N.J.: Prentice-Hall, 1978), 6–13.
9. For discussions of conventional and unconventional political activities, see Samuel H. Barnes and Max Kaase, eds., *Political Action* (Beverly Hills, Calif.: Sage, 1979).
10. Ibid., 87–92.
11. Bureau of the Census, *Voting and Registration in the Election of November, 1988*, ser. P-20, no. 435 (Washington, D.C.: Government Printing Office, 1989).
12. Checking the reported turnout of persons interviewed against that recorded in local election-board records, the Center for Political Studies, like the Census Bureau, has found that citizens tend to overreport their voting participation. Citizens are less likely to falsely report engaging in other forms of political participation, because they are not under the pressure of cultural norms to engage in them. For discussions of overreporting of voting turnout and its

consequences for political analysis, see Aage Clausen, "Response Validity: Vote Report," *Public Opinion Quarterly* 32 (1968): 588–606; John P. Katosh and Michael W. Traugott, "The Consequences of Validated and Self-Reported Voting Measures," *Public Opinion Quarterly* 45 (1981): 519–535; and Paul R. Abramson and William Claggett, "Race-Related Differences in Self-Reported and Validated Turnout," *Journal of Politics* 46 (1984): 719–738; "Race-Related Differences in Self-Reported and Validated Turnout in 1984," *Journal of Politics* 48 (May 1986): 412–422; "Race-Related Differences in Self-Reported and Validated Turnout in 1986," *Journal of Politics* 51 (May 1989): 397–408.

13. Kenneth Mackenzie, *The English Parliament* (Harmondsworth, U.K.: Penguin, 1959), 97–102.

14. Dudley O. McGovney, *The American Suffrage Medley* (Chicago: University of Chicago Press, 1949), chap. 1. See also Kirk Harold Porter, *A History of Suffrage in the United States* (New York: AMS, 1971).

15. Charles E. Johnson, Jr., *Nonvoting Americans,* Bureau of the Census, Current Population Reports, ser. P-23, no. 102 (Washington, D.C.: Government Printing Office, 1980), 2 (table A).

16. U.S. Department of Commerce, Bureau of the Census, *Registration and Voting in the November, 1988, Election,* Series P-20, no. 440 (Washington, D.C.: Government Printing Office, October 1989), table A. Using calculations based on election returns compiled from various sources, the 1988 turnout was 50.1 percent of the voting-age population. See U.S. Department of Commerce, Bureau of the Census, "Projections of the Voting Age Population for States, November 1990," Series P-25, No. 1059 (Washington, D.C.: U.S. Government Printing Office, April 1990), 19, table 5.

17. Johnson, *Nonvoting Americans,* 5, table B, and 7, fig. 4; *Voting and Registration in the Election of November, 1988,* table A; and U.S. Department of Commerce, *Statistical Abstract of the United States, 1982–1983,* 489, table 801.

18. It was learned that these four persons were funded by Republican President Richard Nixon's campaign committee, the Committee to Re-elect the President. Other illegal activities, conducted by Nixon's campaign committee or by the White House itself, included unauthorized wiretappings, other burglaries sponsored by White House staff members, illegal contributions to Nixon's campaign committee, and illegal expenditures on its behalf. For a full history of these events, see William B. Dickerson, Jr., ed., *Watergate: Chronology of a Crisis* (Washington, D.C.: CQ Press, 1973).

19. For discussions of the roles of symbols and rituals in politics, see Murray Edelman, *The Symbolic Uses of Politics* (Urbana: University of Illinois Press, 1964); Murray Edelman, *Politics as Symbolic Action* (Chicago: Marham, 1971); and Charles D. Elder and Roger W. Cobb, *The Political Uses of Symbols* (New York: Longman, 1983).

20. Alexander T. Edelman, *Latin American Government and Politics* (Homewood, Ill.: Dorsey, 1969), 377.

21. Ibid.

Chapter 2

Social Characteristics and Patterns of Political Participation

The extent to which citizens participate in politics and the ways in which they do so are structured by their social circumstances. These circumstances include how individuals live, the kinds of neighborhoods they live in, how much and what kinds of education they have, the kinds of work they do and how much they earn, and the opportunities they have for improving their lives. Social circumstances affect the level of resources available for political participation and serve to foster or inhibit development of the attitudes and beliefs that underlie various types of political participation. Indicators of social circumstances include such characteristics as age, race, education, sex, region and place of residence, marital status, and social class (of individuals and of their parents).[1]

Life experiences, which are in part determined by social circumstances, also influence citizens' patterns of political behavior. For example, individuals who have been poor are likely to value economic security more than those who have never known poverty.[2] Life experiences, with their resultant evaluations of the past and expectations about the future, vary according to such factors as social class, race, gender, ethnicity, educational attainment, employment patterns, and career choice.[3]

Differences in life experiences are not constant over time. For example, the range of occupations open to women has increased dramatically in recent years. Entry into occupations formerly closed to them has affected many aspects of women's lives, including their educational choices, career opportunities, and income levels. As a result it has changed many aspects of their roles and status in society.[4] Political issues reflect life experiences that are particularly important to large segments of the electorate. As life experiences change with economic and social conditions, their effects on citizens' political views and mobilization for political activity also change.

Several alternative explanations for the effects of social characteristics on political participation can be offered. One is that they affect the social roles that people play, influencing both the expectations people apply to others and those they apply to themselves.[5] Another explanation is that placement in the social structure affects the flow of political communications, with individuals in some social locations receiving more political stimuli than others. Exposure to higher levels of political information stimulates political interest and involvement and increases political activity.

A third explanation is that position in the social structure affects both citizens' stakes in political outcomes and their perceptions of those stakes. While all citizens are affected by governmental decisions, not all perceive equally clearly the extent to which those decisions affect their interests. For example, middle-class citizens receive many direct benefits from government programs, such as insured mortgage loans, grants and low-interest loans to help pay their children's college expenses, and income-tax deductions for such things as interest payments on mortgage loans, real estate property taxes, and contributions to retirement-pension plans. Lower-income people also benefit from a number of government programs: among others, housing subsidies and assistance in the purchase of food and other necessities and in the payment of medical expenses. Both middle-income and lower-income citizens also receive benefits from the government that are provided to the community as a whole—public elementary and secondary schools, public safety services, transportation facilities (roads, highways, and public transit), and parks and recreation facilities. However, awareness of the connection between political participation, government programs, and the quantity and quality of government benefits and services provided is lower among lower-income groups. Groups conducting voter registration and mobilization drives among citizens of lower social status often find that political education is necessary to help them see the connections between political activity and benefits received.[6]

The political attitudes that citizens have also vary with their social characteristics, and certain attitudes are highly related to political participation. Citizens who have higher levels of political interest and involvement, who believe that politicians and the government are responsive to citizens' wishes, who are more trusting of public officials, and who perceive the government as being responsive to their demands are more likely to participate in politics.[7] Those who identify with a political party are also more likely to participate.[8] All these attitudes vary with social characteristics.[9]

This chapter will examine in detail the relationships between several social characteristics and forms of political participation.

Age and Its Correlates

Although citizens between the ages of thirty and sixty-five appear to vote at higher rates than do those who are either older or younger, that is only because of the effects of other social characteristics; when these are controlled, voter turnout increases with age.[10] How can this pattern be explained? Age groups differ in educational attainment and income. Differences in sex-role socialization cause political participation to vary more among women of different ages than among men. Women who became eligible to vote when the 19th Amendment to the Constitution was ratified (1920) or shortly afterward tended to vote at much lower rates than did women who became eligible to vote later.[11] Persons living with a spouse are more likely to vote than those who are single, divorced, or widowed; and because elderly men are more likely to be living with a spouse than are elderly women, elderly men vote at a higher rate. The effects of sex and marital status are thus confounded with those of age.

A "life-cycle effects" theory offers one explanation for why voting turnout does not decline with age when marital status and gender are held constant. Those who previously were occupied with jobs and raising families are free of these burdens during their retirement years. Thus, many other interests and distractions that existed earlier would be eliminated or reduced, so these citizens could devote more of their attention to politics.

There is evidence that refutes this explanation, however. The explanation implies that housewives would vote less than employed women in the same age category, since working women would be expected to be better informed and to perceive better the impact of government policies on their interests. While some studies report this to be the case,[12] a survey based on a very large sample, conducted by the Bureau of the Census, found that during the 1970s housewives voted at the same rates as did women who worked outside the home.[13] Furthermore, differences in turnout levels among different occupational groups (including the occupation of housewife) are influenced more by their levels of educational attainment than by their occupation.[14]

The attitudes that are significant in motivating voting participation also vary significantly by age group. Older persons are less likely to perceive the government as being responsive to citizens,[15] but they are more likely to identify strongly with one of the two major political parties.[16] Compared to their opposites, persons who do not perceive the government as responsive are less likely to vote, but persons with strong party identification are more likely to vote.[17]

Older citizens as a group have lower levels of education. Individuals who are more educated are more likely to vote and to engage in other forms of political activity. Therefore, on the basis of educational attainment we would expect older citizens to have lower levels of political participation.[18]

The effects of age on participation can also be seen in a study of parents of former high school students, who were interviewed in 1965 and reinterviewed in 1973 and again in 1982. At the beginning of the seventeen-year period, the parents had an average age of fifty-three, while in 1982 the average age was seventy. In 1982 the parents' level of political knowledge remained approximately the same as in 1965, but their sense of political effectiveness and frequency of reading about politics in newspapers had declined, while their ideological sophistication had increased. The proportion of this group engaging in most forms of active participation declined over the period; fewer reported trying to influence others how to vote, attending political meetings, displaying signs or wearing campaign buttons, and engaging in other political acts. Most of the decline in participation can be accounted for by a decrease in participation by those over the age of sixty-five and by a disenchantment with politics that occurred between 1973 and 1982. Many of the political activities reported were of specific appeal to older citizens; these included attending meetings related to senior citizens' problems, reading a newspaper column for senior citizens, and going to a senior citizens' center.[19]

Younger citizens are less likely to participate than are middle-aged citizens. Several social characteristics interact with age to produce this effect. One is marital status: a lower proportion of those who are under the age of twenty-five are married, and persons who are not married are less likely to be involved in politics. Interpersonal influences have a significant impact on voting participation among those less interested in politics, with the influence of one's spouse being particularly important.[20] A second reason why young citizens participate in politics less is their high rate of mobility. Individuals who have lived in an area for a relatively short time are less likely to vote, and younger citizens move more frequently than do older citizens.[21]

The legal consequences of mobility are potentially less of an inhibitor to voting participation now than in the past. Previously, many states had lengthy residency requirements for eligibility to vote, but in the aftermath of several court decisions, residency requirements are no longer a serious obstacle to voting. Many states do close their voter registration books before elections, and this could be a problem for those who have very recently moved to those states. However, no state closes its registration books more than fifty days before an election.

It is, rather, the social consequences of mobility that are now important. Those who have not lived in a community for very long usually have fewer social and organizational ties, less information about local issues, and fewer political contacts, and they are less interested in and involved in the local community. These effects of mobility are greater on middle-aged persons who move, but those who are younger move more frequently.[22]

Citizen participation increases markedly among persons who have lived in a community for three to five years. It may be that such a length of residence is necessary for acclimation to the community and for development of an interest in its problems and politics. Another explanation is that national politics in the form of the presidential election campaign stimulates sufficient political interest among community newcomers that they will register to vote and become more politically active in other ways.[23]

The role of community ties in political participation is evident when voting turnout rates among college students are compared with those of nonstudents of the same age group. Community norms within the college student community usually promote voting participation; social interaction and integration into the campus community further encourage participation among students. Special efforts may be made to register students on the campus itself, thereby lowering the costs of registering, in time and effort, to the students. Among nonstudents, community norms and peer pressure frequently are less supportive of participation, and voter registration may require more individual initiative and effort. After students leave the college environment, a drop in political participation rates occurs.[24]

Controversy exists about the impact of the assumption of adult roles on the political participation rates of younger citizens. One view is that participation increases as young people take up adult roles and responsibilities. In this view, young parents become concerned with the schools, recreational facilities, and other community amenities as their children reach school age, and their increased concern leads to more participation. Thus, one hypothesis is that married younger citizens would have higher rates of voting turnout than would single people, and voting turnout is higher (by 3 to 5 percent) among young married people than among single people of the same age.[25]

In summary, patterns of political participation by citizens of different ages are influenced by other social characteristics that reflect variations in life experiences. Among older citizens, women and those who are single and who have lower levels of education are less likely to participate in politics. Among younger citizens, those who have moved more recently, are not currently in college, or are not married are less likely to be political participants.

Components of Socioeconomic Status

Socioeconomic status is of paramount importance to both the type and the frequency of political activities engaged in by citizens in the United States. Citizens of higher socioeconomic status are more likely to engage in several different kinds of political activities, including organizational and campaign activities and contacting public officials as well as voting in elections.[26] They also perform each of these activities more frequently. This pattern of more frequent performance of several types of political activity by persons of higher socioeconomic status does not occur in all developed democracies. In some countries, social and political organizations mobilize individuals of lower socioeconomic status and bring them to levels of political activity similar to those attained by the middle class.[27]

One explanation for the more frequent political activity by persons of higher socioeconomic status is that they possess higher levels of politically relevant resources.[28] Other explanations stress greater access to political information, higher levels of capacity to process that information, and greater awareness of the impact of political decisions on their interests. Persons of higher socioeconomic status are also more likely to have the civic orientations—such as perceptions of government responsiveness and sense of obligation to participate—that motivate citizens to participate in politics.[29]

What is it about high socioeconomic status that stimulates higher rates of political participation? Social status is usually measured by an index that combines two or three of the main components of social status—education, occupation, and income. It may help us to understand how socioeconomic status has its effects on participation if we analyze the effects of each of these three components separately.

TABLE 2-1
Reported Voter Turnout by Education, 1952–1988
(percent who say they voted in the most recent election)

Level of educational attainment	Presidential elections									
	1952	1956	1960	1964	1968	1972	1976	1980	1984	1988
Grade school	62.1	60.3	67.3	67.8	60.4	58.0	59.8	58.6	58.0	41.7
High school	80.1	74.4	81.1	77.8	78.3	70.1	60.0	54.8	66.3	58.2
College	89.5	89.7	90.3	88.2	84.1	86.6	85.0	76.4	85.5	82.4

	Midterm elections							
	1958	1962	1966	1970	1974	1978	1982	1986
Grade school	48.9	51.1	52.4	49.3	43.6	47.8	44.5	36.2
High school	56.4	59.8	61.7	55.9	57.8	48.0	54.2	51.0
College	73.2	71.9	74.2	76.7	65.5	66.9	70.8	72.1

SOURCES: Data for 1952–1978 from Warren E. Miller, Arthur H. Miller, and Edward J. Schneider, *American National Election Studies Data Sourcebook, 1952–1978* (Cambridge: Harvard University Press, 1980), table 5.23. Copyright © 1980 by the President and Fellows of Harvard College; used by permission. Data for 1980, 1982, 1984, 1986, and 1988 from the American National Election Studies, Center for Political Studies, University of Michigan.

Education

Education is the most important component of socioeconomic status in influencing political participation in the United States. Individuals who have higher levels of education not only vote more often (see Table 2-1), but also they participate more by working in campaigns and taking part in organizational and other activities. Even among individuals within the same income level, those who have more education participate more.[30]

The importance of education to participation arises from several sources. Those who have more education generally know more about how the political system works; therefore, they are more aware of the consequences of government actions for their lives. Those who are more educated are also more likely to live in a social environment in which considerable social pressure exists to be politically active, at least to the extent of voting. These social norms may also have been instilled by parents; those who have higher levels of education tend to come from families in which the parents had higher levels of education as well.[31]

Education also imparts certain skills that facilitate participation in politics. For example, anyone who has dealt successfully with the bureaucratic structure and procedures of a large university has developed the skills necessary to handle successfully the bureaucratic tasks involved in voter registration. Education also helps develop the skills required for engaging in other political activities, such as running for office, serving as an officer in a political party, taking a leadership role in a political campaign, or serving as an officer in an organization (union or local civic group) that becomes involved in campaigns or lobbying activity.

Education is also associated with acquiring higher levels of the kinds of cognitive skills that facilitate political activity. These include the reading and analytical skills that enable individuals to understand complex events and problems and to understand the connections among them. Higher levels of education may also stimulate increased political interest, which in turn leads to increased participation.[32] Individuals who are more interested in politics are more likely to care about the outcome of elections and also to vote and to engage in other political activities.

Citizens who have higher levels of education are more likely to follow political events in the mass media,[33] and especially in the print media. The print media, both newspapers and news magazines, present far more information about national political events than can be covered in a half-hour television newscast. Comprehensive coverage of local and state political events and policy decisions also is usually provided only in a local newspaper, although the quality of the coverage varies substantially from one paper to another.

Those who have higher levels of educational attainment are more likely to have opinions on a wide range of subjects and are therefore more easily stimulated to engage in political activity. Those who are more educated are also more likely to engage in discussions with others about politics and to feel free to discuss politics with a wider range of people. More educated citizens are also more likely to believe that they can, through their actions, have an impact on the government.[34]

Educational attainment also affects attitudes toward others and participation in organized groups. Citizens with more education are more likely to express confidence in their social environment and in their ability to have an impact in changing elements of their environment with which they are not satisfied.[35] One aspect of this is that individuals with higher levels of educational attainment are more likely to perceive the government as responsive to their interests and their activities.[36] The percentage of the electorate in each educational category has varied over time since the 1950s, but the relationship between education and turnout has persisted.

Differences also exist in the extent to which citizens overreport voting turnout. The expectations that individuals believe others have about them influence reports of voting turnout. For example, individuals who are more highly educated, have a stronger sense of civic duty and partisan identification, feel more politically efficacious, and have greater concern with election outcomes are more likely to overreport voting, because they are more likely to believe that others expect them to vote. Black citizens who live in predominantly black areas and who are interviewed by black interviewers are also more likely to overreport voting than are white citizens. When voting turnout is validated by checking reported turnout against election board records, differences in turnout rates between whites and blacks remain, even when comparing within the same level of education and controlling for the region in which the citizens live.[37] Thus, in addition to other factors discussed, perceptions of others' expectations influence levels of political participation.

Income

Within each level of educational attainment, those who have higher incomes tend to participate more, though the differences are small.[38] Several explanations can be offered for the effects of income. First, the poor must focus a disproportionate amount of their attention on obtaining the necessities of life, which means they have less time and energy for politics. For those in lower income brackets, political activity might be regarded as a "luxury" item.

Second, citizens who have higher incomes are likely to live and work in environments that stimulate interest in politics, create social pressures for political participation, and provide opportunities for political participation.[39] Political interest is for many individuals stimulated by the information made available to them through their jobs. That information may include political knowledge as well as details of how government activity affects the business or the sector of the economy in which they are employed. Persons in higher income groups may also be more exposed to information about how government policies affect various aspects of personal life, such as tax obligations, conditions of employment, and environmental quality.

Finally, some effects of higher income are related to personal characteristics. Individuals who succeed financially (especially those without higher levels of education) probably have other personal attributes that might be expected to stimulate greater political activity. These include personality traits conducive to higher levels of activity and personal competence and a tendency to pay greater attention to events outside their immediate personal environment.[40]

Occupation

Once differences in political participation attributable to education have been taken into account, very few effects of occupation remain. However, for three occupational categories, participation rates are higher than what would be predicted by educational level; these categories are farm ownership, clerical and sales work, and government employment.[41]

The income and job security of both farm owners and government employees are directly and significantly affected by governmental activities. Most farmers produce commodities that receive some form of government subsidy or are grown under some form of quota system. Changes in subsidies or quotas can substantially alter the level of farm incomes. In addition, a substantial proportion of American agricultural production is exported, and export levels are strongly influenced by international trade agreements, foreign-exchange rates, and governmental regulation of trade in agricultural products. Furthermore, a substantial proportion of American farmers borrow money to finance their operations, so that interest-rate levels have a major effect on their ability to make a profit—and these interest rates are largely determined by the government's monetary and fiscal policies. Farm owners are well aware of these facts and consequently have much higher rates of political participation than would be predicted from their other sociodemographic characteristics.[42]

Government employees also have high rates of voting turnout.[43] Those for whom other forms of political participation are not prohibited under civil service and merit systems are also likely to engage in other types of participation at rates beyond what would be predicted by their levels of education. Government employees tend to have high levels of political interest, to be more knowledgeable about politics, to follow politics more in the mass media, and to have a higher sense of civic duty. Those who are not covered by merit systems are sometimes expected to engage in political activity as a condition of continued employment, although some research suggests that such expectations are not as important as they were thirty or forty years ago.[44]

One explanation for the higher participation rates of clerical and sales workers is that their jobs require them to deal with abstractions and to cope with bureaucratic forms. They either have or develop the verbal and communications skills that facilitate their understanding of political events and their participation in political activities.[45]

Some have argued that one major difference in occupations that affects participation is the amount of free time they allow for following political events and for participating in political activities. Analyses of the time demands of different occupations and the use of leisure time in the United States do not sustain such an argument: neither blue-collar workers who work a forty-hour week nor the unemployed are more likely to participate than are those whose occupations require that substantially more hours be devoted to their jobs.[46]

Indeed, unemployment seems to have the opposite effect on political participation. Individuals who are unemployed tend to focus their attention on personal economic concerns, withdrawing from politics.[47] Financial resources that could be allocated to political activity are not likely to be available.[48] When other variables—such as age, gender, education, usual occupation, and length of residence—are controlled, those who have been unemployed (or who, for whatever reason, feel that they are financially worse off than they had been previously) are less likely to vote.[49]

Other Social Characteristics

Race

Equal access to the ballot box and equal opportunity to participate in politics in other ways did not effectively exist for persons of minority races in many areas of this country until the mid-1960s. Voter-registration laws and procedures in some states discouraged political participation by citizens in general

TABLE 2-2

Reported Registration and Turnout by Race, 1966–1988

Year	Presidential elections					Midterm elections			
	Percent registered		Percent voting		Year	Percent registered		Percent voting	
	White	Black	White	Black		White	Black	White	Black
1968	75.4	66.2	69.1	57.6	1966	71.7	66.2	64.5	52.1
1972	73.4	65.5	64.5	52.1	1970	69.1	60.8	56.0	43.5
1976	68.3	58.5	60.9	48.7	1974	63.5	54.9	46.3	33.8
1980	68.4	60.0	60.9	50.5	1978	63.8	57.1	47.3	37.2
1984	69.6	66.3	61.4	55.8	1982	65.6	59.1	49.9	43.0
1988	67.9	64.5	59.1	51.5	1986	65.3	64.0	47.0	43.2

SOURCES: U.S. Department of Commerce, Bureau of the Census, "Voter Participation in November 1972," Series P-20, No. 244 (Washington: Government Printing Office, December 1972), tables A and B; "Voting and Registration in the Election of November 1988," Series P-20, No. 440 (Washington: Government Printing Office, October 1989), tables A and B.

but usually had their strongest impact on those of minority races. Among these laws and procedures were the closing of voter registration books months before an election, irregular hours for registration and lack of evening and Saturday registration hours, and inadequate provisions for absentee registration. It has been estimated that improvements in just these procedural aspects would have increased voter turnout in the South by 14.5 percent among blacks and 12.4 percent among whites.[50] Beyond these procedural obstacles, political participation by minority-race members was inhibited in some areas of the South especially by discriminatory administration of the laws and even by threats of physical violence or economic retaliation against blacks who attempted to register to vote. Beginning in 1957, the enactment of a number of civil-rights laws, the issuing of several important court decisions, and the passage of the 24th Amendment (abolishing poll-tax requirements) have gone a long way toward providing access to the ballot box to all citizens in all areas of the country.[51]

Racial patterns of voter turnout for the twelve elections from 1966 to 1988 are shown in Table 2-2. Black citizens were less likely than white citizens to report being registered and voting in the general election. A decline in registration and turnout among both groups occurred after 1966, but the decline was steeper among whites than among blacks in both presidential and midterm elections.

Black citizens were less likely than whites to vote before the enactment of the Voting Rights Act of 1965. In 1952, only 4 percent of southern blacks of voting age voted, compared to 64 percent of nonsouthern blacks. Turnout among southern blacks increased to 31 percent in 1960 and to 63 percent in 1968. Among nonsouthern blacks, 83 percent voted in 1964, but turnout in this group then declined slightly. Among both southern and nonsouthern whites, turnout increased from 1952 to 1960, then declined through 1972; however, the decline was greater among northern whites than among those residing in the south.[52]

Because of previously restricted educational opportunities, a lower proportion of minority-race citizens have completed college or high school. However, while controls for the effects of

level of education and region reduce the disparity in voter turnout between blacks and whites, black citizens are nevertheless
less likely to vote than are white citizens of the same socioeconomic status.[53]

Among younger black voters (eighteen to twenty-four), turnout was at its highest level in 1964. Turnout declined from 1968
through 1980, then increased in 1984. In that year, 40.6 percent
reported voting, partly as a consequence of presidential candidate Jesse Jackson's voter mobilization efforts in unsuccessful
pursuit of the Democratic party's nomination. In 1988, young
black citizens' participation declined again, falling to 35 percent
who reported casting a presidential ballot.[54]

Variables may not have the same influence on members of
different groups. Groups differ in the extent to which members
identify with them; higher levels of group consciousness stimulate higher levels of voting turnout among the members of some
groups but not others. For example, research suggests that black
consciousness stimulated higher rates of voting participation, in
comparison to whites of the same age groups, among older black
southerners in 1984.[55]

Ethnicity

Hispanic citizens have lower rates of turnout and other forms
of political participation than do either white or black citizens.
There is only limited evidence on the causes of these low levels
of participation. Among the explanations offered is the language
barrier. Another factor may be the age distribution of Hispanics
in the United States: Chicano (Mexican American) and Puerto
Rican groups have a relatively high proportion of younger citizens, and as already noted, younger citizens are less likely to
participate in politics. Levels of educational attainment are also
lower among Hispanics than among the rest of the population.
Within socioeconomic status levels, however, Chicanos are slightly
more likely to vote than is the rest of the Hispanic citizenry.[56]
On the other hand, Puerto Ricans are slightly less likely to vote.
One explanation given for this is that many Puerto Ricans, in-
tending to return to Puerto Rico, view their stay on the U.S.

mainland as temporary. As a consequence, they do not become involved in politics.[57] In contrast to these two Hispanic groups, Cuban Americans tend to be older, better educated, and more affluent, and they participate at higher rates.[58]

Research conducted in California shows that Hispanic and Asian American citizens are less likely to participate politically than white or black citizens; this applies to all forms of participation. Political participation among Asian American citizens varies by nationality: Japanese, Korean, and Filipino Americans are less likely to register and vote than are white Americans; Chinese Americans are equally likely to register and vote as are white Americans. Members of Asian American ethnic groups are less likely to contact public officials than are whites, but Japanese Americans are more likely to contribute money than are whites. When controls are applied for sociodemographic characteristics and group identifications, ethnicity remains an important variable for Asian Americans, but not for black or Hispanic Americans. In other words, sociodemographic variables account for differences in participation levels between whites and blacks or Latinos.[59]

One study indicates that noncitizens (both Asian American and Hispanic) engage in political participation to a limited extent through working in groups (11 percent), contacting the media (15 percent), and contacting officials (18 percent); length of time spent in the United States is the most important factor in accounting for participation. Noncitizens are more likely to participate in a group if they believe they have a problem related to their ethnicity, such as access to the educational system or perceived inadequacy of public services available in their residential area.[60]

Gender

In the past, women have participated less than men in politics, regardless of whether participation was measured in terms of voting, campaign and party work, running for public office, or community-oriented activities. Survey data available since 1952 show that the differences in voter turnout, although lower in

TABLE 2-3

Reported Voter Turnout by Gender, 1952–1988

(percent who say they voted in the most recent election)

Year	Men	Women
1952	79.7	69.3
1956	79.5	67.6
1958	66.7	49.6
1960	84.1	74.7
1962	63.7	57.7
1964	80.2	75.6
1966	65.1	59.9
1968	78.1	74.1
1970	61.9	57.5
1972	76.4	70.1
1974	56.2	49.9
1976	76.9	67.8
1978	55.3	53.9
1980	73.3	69.8
1982	63.1	58.1
1984	73.6	73.6
1986	52.8	52.3
1988	72.2	67.8

SOURCES: Data for 1952–1978 from Warren E. Miller, Arthur H. Miller, and Edward J. Schneider, *American National Election Studies Sourcebook* (Cambridge: Harvard University Press, 1980), table 5.23. Copyright © 1980 by the President and Fellows of Harvard College; used by permission. Data for 1980, 1982, 1984, 1986, and 1988 from the American National Election Studies, Center for Political Studies, University of Michigan.

recent years than during the 1950s, remain in the range of 5 to 10 percentage points (see Table 2-3). However, when age and level of educational attainment are held constant, by the late 1970s college-educated women, and particularly those in their thirties and younger, were as likely to vote as were their male counterparts.[61]

Surveys conducted in 1967 and 1976 indicate that women are becoming more active in local politics—joining with others to form or run an organization seeking to solve a local problem, attending school board or city council meetings, and contacting local public officials. In 1967, only college-educated women tended to participate in such activities as much as men with the same level of education. By 1976, women with a high-school education were also as likely as men with a comparable level of education to participate in these activities.[62]

Differences in campaign activity are also diminishing, but they remain substantial. Comparison of the average number of campaign-related acts performed showed that women were less active than men in every presidential election from 1952 to 1972,[63] and an examination of specific campaign activities performed in 1980, even after controlling for level of education, indicated that women were still less active than men.[64] Several explanations can be offered for the lower rates of campaign participation by women. One is that women pay less attention to politics; for example, they are substantially less likely to follow politics in the mass media.[65] Leisure-time studies suggest that working women have less time to keep up with political news, because they usually have almost total responsibility for household tasks and family care.[66]

Women are also less likely to have high levels of certain attitudes and beliefs that are associated with political participation. These include a belief that one can understand politics and government and that political events can be influenced by activities of individuals like oneself (this attitude is called *internal political efficacy*). Another important attitude is that public officials are responsive to the interests of individuals like oneself and that governmental and political institutions, such as legislatures and political parties, help make the government responsive to people like oneself (*external political efficacy*). Another attitude that is significantly related to levels of political participation is *governmental attentiveness:* the belief that various governmental and political institutions respond favorably to the policy preferences of the general public. While women tend to have levels of external political efficacy equivalent to those of men, women have substantially lower levels of internal efficacy. That is, they are less likely to perceive that people like themselves can influence the activities of the government. Women also perceive the government as less attentive and responsive to citizens' preferences than do men.[67]

What are the sources of these attitudes? One is probably childhood socialization of girls to the view that interest and activity in politics are more appropriate for males. Research in the 1950s and 1960s found that girls were both less interested in politics and less knowledgeable about governmental and political processes and events. Some later studies report fewer and smaller differences between boys and girls in both knowledge and attitudes, so that if there is a link between childhood socialization and adult levels of political participation, higher rates of participation could be expected among women coming to adulthood in the 1980s and later. However, the evidence on this question is not conclusive.[68]

Another explanation may be women's traditional adult roles. Persons who are not employed outside the home may be less interested in politics, acquire less politically relevant information, be less likely to perceive the consequences of political events for their own and their family's well-being, and be less likely to develop the skills necessary for successful political activism. Even when women have been employed outside the home, their occupations have traditionally been restricted to a few categories, such as teaching, secretarial and clerical work, and nursing; they have only infrequently been employed in occupations, such as business and the law, from which political activists are often recruited. The barriers to employment were lowered during the 1970s, and more women are now employed in the latter kinds of occupations.[69] Some research supports the view that those who are employed outside the home are more likely to participate in politics,[70] although employment patterns may not be related to voting turnout.[71]

Another explanation that has been offered for the lower rates of participation among women is that the men who serve as gatekeepers in the political process have negative attitudes toward women's participation. While women's willingness to perform the menial tasks of campaign work has made them an important part of the campaign work force during the past three decades, only recently has their engagement in higher-level political and campaign tasks been more favorably received.[72] These negative attitudes persist among male political leaders in many areas of the country, particularly toward women as candidates for elective office. Thus, women frequently face great difficulties in obtaining the political-party and interest-group organizational and financial support that is necessary for a successful candidacy.[73]

Increases in all forms of political participation among women can be expected. Changes in women's educational attainment, in their employment and their occupational and other roles, in their attitudes, and in the attitudes of the public all tend in that direction. Media attention to women who are active in politics presents younger women with political role models. Women will also learn the skills necessary for political activity and acquire the necessary resources as more of them move into the occupations of business and law, from which elected public officials are commonly recruited.

Summary

Political participation varies with the life experiences of citizens. As these life experiences change, patterns of political participation change. Participation varies widely with social status, the most important component of which is educational attainment. Those who have more years of formal education are more likely to engage in all forms of political activity. Occupation also has an impact, with individuals in certain occupations being more likely to participate than would be predicted on the basis of educational attainment or income. These occupations are either heavily impacted by government policies or provide skills necessary for political participation. There have also been gender differences, but changes in the life circumstances of women during the past two decades, particularly in educational attainment and patterns of employment, are being accompanied by changes in their patterns of political participation. Racial and ethnic differences have also existed, with minority-group members participating less than members of the white majority. In large part these differences can be accounted for by lower levels of educational attainment and by deliberate efforts to discourage political participation by minority-group members. The legal barriers to political participation have largely been removed, and rising educational attainment and other changes have been accompanied by increased rates of political participation among minority-group members. Thus, it is reasonable to expect increasing similarities in political participation among members of different ethnic and racial groups and between the sexes in the future. However, differences in participation patterns based on social status, age, and marital status do not appear likely to change.

One question that must be addressed is why turnout has declined since 1960, when the educational attainment, income, and occupational status levels of citizens have increased substantially during the intervening years; recall that higher levels of income, education, and occupation are associated with higher levels of participation. One answer is that there are offsetting changes in other characteristics of the American electorate. Thus, while more citizens are better educated, hold higher-status occupations, and have higher levels of income, a greater proportion also are in younger age groups, are more geographically mobile, and are not married—all characteristics that are associated with lower levels of voting turnout. In addition, their sociopolitical characteristics—such as having a party identification, holding party identification strongly, reading about politics and government in newspapers frequently, and having a strong sense of political efficacy—have declined. The decline in these sociopolitical variables more than offsets the increases in those associated with higher levels of turnout. In the next chapter we will examine the patterns of change in political attitudes that are related to political participation.[74]

NOTES

1. See Sidney Verba and Norman H. Nie, *Participation in America* (New York: Harper and Row, 1972), chap. 1. For a different formulation of the link between social circumstances and participation, see William Mishler, *Political Participation in Canada* (Toronto: Macmillan, 1979), 104–108.
2. See the following works by Ronald Inglehart: *The Silent Revolution* (Princeton: Princeton University Press, 1977); "The Changing Structure of Political Cleavages in Western Society," in *Electoral Change in Advanced Industrial Democracies*, ed. Russell Dalton, Scott Flanagan, and Paul Beck (Princeton: Princeton University Press, 1984); "Aggregate Stability and Individual-Level Change in Mass Belief Systems: The Level of Analysis Paradox," *American Political Science Review* 79 (1985): 79–116; "New Perspectives on Value Change," *Comparative Political Studies* 17 (1985): 485–532; *Culture Shift in Advanced Industrial Societies* (Princeton: Princeton University Press, 1990).

   For a criticism of Inglehart's methods and measures, see Scott Flanagan, "Changing Values in Advanced Industrial Societies," *Comparative Political Studies* 14 (1982): 403–444; and "Measuring Value Change in Advanced Industrial Societies," *Comparative Political Studies* 15 (1982): 99–128. For a debate over the appropriateness of Inglehart's conclusions about value change in western democracies, see Ronald Inglehart and Scott Flanagan, "Controversies: Value Change in Industrial Societies," *American Political Science Review* 81 (1987): 1289–1319.

3. See, for example, Robert E. Lane, *Political Life* (Glencoe, Ill.: Free Press, 1959), and the works cited in n. 1. See also William H. Chafe, *Women and Equality* (New York: Oxford University Press, 1977); and Paul C. Light, *Baby Boomers* (New York: W. W. Norton, 1988); Kay Lehman Schlozman and Sidney Verba, *Insult to Injury* (Cambridge: Harvard University Press, 1979); Reeve Vanneman and Lynn Weber Cannon, *The American Perception of Class* (Philadelphia: Temple University Press, 1987).

4. Barbara Sinclair Deckard, *The Women's Movement*, 3d ed. (New York: Harper and Row, 1983), chaps. 6, 7, 11, and 12; and Nancy McGlen and Karen O'Connor, *Women's Rights: The Struggle for Equality in the Nineteenth and Twentieth Centuries* (New York: Praeger, 1983), chaps. 5 and 6.

5. For example, individuals of higher socioeconomic status are expected to vote. When they do not, they have violated the role expectations that they and others hold. Thus, when interviewed after an election, citizens of higher social status who have not voted are more likely to claim that they have voted than are citizens of lower social status. See Kenneth Grant and L. John Roos, "Measuring Participation Using Public Opinion Surveys: Who Lies and Why" (paper delivered at the annual meeting of the Midwest Political Science Association, Chicago, 1983).

6. See the manual written for this purpose by Debra R. Livingston, *Power at the Polls* (Silver Spring, Md.: National Association of Social Workers, 1983), 21.

7. Warren E. Miller, "Disinterest, Disaffection, and Participation in Presidential Politics," *Political Behavior* 26 (1980): 7–32; and Carol Cassell and David Hill, "The Decision to Vote," in *Public Opinion and Public Policy*, ed. N. Luttbeg (Itasca, Ill.: Peacock, 1981), 46–53.

8. Paul R. Abramson and John H. Aldrich, "The Decline of Electoral Participation in America," *American Political Science Review* 76 (1982): 502–521.

9. Warren E. Miller and Santa A. Traugott, *American National Election Studies Data Sourcebook, 1952–1986* (Cambridge: Harvard University Press, 1989), 273, table 4.38, 282, table 4.47, 305, table 5.23, 309, table 5.28.

10. Raymond E. Wolfinger and Steven J. Rosenstone, *Who Votes?* (New Haven: Yale University Press, 1980).

11. John J. Stucker, "Women as Voters: Their Maturation as Political Persons in American Society," in *A Portrait of Marginality*, ed. M. Githens and J. Prestage (New York: McKay, 1977), 264–283; McGlen and O'Connor, *Women's Rights*, chap. 4; Virginia Sapiro, *The Political Integration of Women* (Urbana: University of Illinois Press, 1983).

12. Kristi Andersen, "Working Women and Political Participation, 1952–1972," *American Journal of Political Science* 19 (1975): 439–454.

13. Wolfinger and Rosenstone, *Who Votes?*, 49.

14. Ibid.

15. Paul Abramson, *Political Attitudes in America* (San Francisco: W. H. Freeman, 1983), 185; Warren E. Miller, Arthur H. Miller, and Edward J. Schneider, *American National Election Studies Data Sourcebook, 1952–1978* (Cambridge: Harvard University Press, 1980), 284, table 4.41.

16. Miller, Miller, and Schneider, *Sourcebook*, 121, table 2.39.

17. Abramson and Aldrich, "Decline," 506–510.

18. Wolfinger and Rosenstone, *Who Votes?*, 37–41.

19. M. Kent Jennings and Gregory Markus, "Political Involvement in the Later Years: A Longitudinal Survey," *American Journal of Political Science* 32 (1988): 302–317.

20. Wolfinger and Rosenstone, *Who Votes?*, 44–46.

21. Ibid., 50–54.
22. Ibid., 51; Peverill Squire, Raymond E. Wolfinger, and David P. Glass, "Residential Mobility and Voter Turnout," *American Political Science Review*, 81 (1987): 45–65; Ann R. Kendrick, "Group Economic Interests and Black Turnout in the 1984 Election" (paper presented at the American Political Science Association meeting, Atlanta, August 31–September 3, 1989).
23. Wolfinger and Rosenstone, *Who Votes?*, 53.
24. Ibid., 56–57.
25. Ibid., 56.
26. Verba and Nie, *Participation*, 132, fig. 8.4; Norman H. Nie, Sidney Verba, Henry E. Brady, Kay Lehman Schlozman, and Jane Junn, "Participation in America: Continuity and Change" (paper presented at the Midwest Political Science Association, Chicago, April 14–16, 1989).
27. See, for example, Sidney Verba, Norman H. Nie, and Jae-on Kim, *Participation and Political Equality* (Cambridge: Cambridge University Press, 1978); Ivor Crewe, "Electoral Participation," in *Democracy at the Polls*, ed. David Butler, Howard R. Penniman, and Austin Ranney (Washington, D.C.: American Enterprise Institute, 1981), 251–253; G. Bingham Powell, *Contemporary Democracies: Participation, Stability, and Violence* (Cambridge: Harvard University Press, 1982), 117–120; G. Bingham Powell, "American Voter Turnout in Comparative Perspective," *American Political Science Review*, 80 (1986): 17–43.
28. Powell, *Contemporary Democracies*, 125. Verba, Nie, and Kim, *Participation and Political Equality*, chaps. 4 and 5, examine how political institutions modify the relationships between resources, motivations, and participation.
29. Richard Brody, "The Puzzle of Political Participation," in *The New American Political System*, ed. A. King (Washington, D.C.: American Enterprise Institute, 1978), 287–324.
30. Wolfinger and Rosenstone, *Who Votes?*, 23–26. While higher levels of educational attainment are related to increased likelihood of voting participation in other developed democracies as well, the effects of education on turnout are not as large in these countries as in the United States. See, for example, Powell, "American Voter Turnout in Comparative Perspective," 28, table 3.
31. Gabriel A. Almond and Sidney Verba, *The Civic Culture: Political Attitudes and Democracy in Five Nations* (Princeton: Princeton University Press, 1963), 379–381.
32. Brody, "Puzzle of Political Participation," 299–301.
33. Miller and Traugott, *Sourcebook*, 301, table 5.18.
34. Almond and Verba, *Civic Culture*, 315–318.
35. Ibid.
36. Miller and Traugott, *Sourcebook*, 305, table 5.23.
37. Paul R. Abramson and William Claggett, "Race-Related Differences in Self-Reported and Validated Turnout," *Journal of Politics* 46 (1984), 719–738; Paul R. Abramson and William Claggett, "Race-Related Differences in Self-Reported and Validated Turnout in 1984," *Journal of Politics* 48 (1986), 412–422; Paul R. Abramson and William Claggett, "Race-Related Differences in Self-Reported and Validated Turnout in 1986," *Journal of Politics* 51 (1989), 397–408; Barbara Anderson, Brian D. Silver, and Paul R. Abramson, "The Effects of Race of the Interviewer on Measures of Electoral Participation by Blacks in SRC National Election Studies," *Public Opinion Quarterly* 52 (1988), 53–83.
38. Wolfinger and Rosenstone, *Who Votes?*, 23.
39. Lester W. Milbrath and M. L. Goel, *Political Participation*, 2d ed. (Chicago: Rand McNally, 1977), 96–98; Lane, *Political Life*, 326–327; Seymour Martin Lipset, *Political Man: The Social Bases of Politics* (Baltimore: Johns Hopkins University Press, 1981), chap. 6; and Giuseppe DiPalma, *Apathy and Participation* (New York: Free Press, 1970), chap. 6.

40. This speculation is offered in Wolfinger and Rosenstone, *Who Votes?*, 21–22.
41. Ibid., 28–34.
42. Michael Lewis-Beck, "Agrarian Political Behavior in the United States," *American Journal of Political Science* 21 (1977): 543–565.
43. Wolfinger and Rosenstone, *Who Votes?*, 95.
44. Frank Sorauf, "State Patronage in a Rural County," *American Political Science Review* 50 (1956): 1046–1056; and Michael Johnston, "Patrons and Clients, Jobs and Machines: A Case Study of the Uses of Patronage," *American Political Science Review* 73 (1979): 385–398.
45. Wolfinger and Rosenstone, *Who Votes?*, 95.
46. For an analysis of time demands, see John Robinson and Philip Converse, "Social Change in the Use of Time," in *The Human Meaning of Social Change*, ed. Angus Campbell and Philip Converse (New York: Russell Sage, 1972), 17–86.
47. Richard A. Brody and Paul M. Sniderman, "From Life Space to the Polling Place: The Relevance of Personal Concerns for Voting Behavior," *British Journal of Political Science* 7 (1977): 344. However, in a study comparing employed and unemployed citizens, Kay L. Schlozman and Sidney Verba found that the unemployed were more likely than the employed to follow politics in the electronic media but less likely to read news in print media. When employment status was included with education, occupation level, race, age, and sex, employment status was not statistically significant in explaining participation (see Schlozman and Verba, *Insult to Injury*, 247, table 9.2) or voting turnout (250, table 9.3). The unemployed are, however, significantly less likely to be registered to vote, even when the effects of other sociodemographic variables are taken into account (253, table 9.5).
48. Schlozman and Verba, *Insult to Injury*, 88.
49. Steven J. Rosenstone, "Economic Adversity and Voting Turnout," *American Journal of Political Science* 26 (1982): 33, table 1.
50. Wolfinger and Rosenstone, *Who Votes?*, 76–79.
51. Richard P. Claude, *The Supreme Court and the Electoral Process* (Baltimore: Johns Hopkins University Press, 1970).
52. Carol Cassel, "Change in Electoral Participation in the South," *Journal of Politics* 41 (1979): 910.
53. Abramson and Claggett, "Race-Related Differences in Self-Reported and Validated Turnout," 719–738.
54. U.S. Dept. of Commerce, Bureau of the Census, "Voting and Registration in the Election of November 1988," Current Population Reports, Series P-20, No. 440 (Washington, D.C.: U.S. Government Printing Office, 1989), 6, table F.
55. Kendrick, "Group Economic Interests and Black Turnout in the 1984 Election."
56. Wolfinger and Rosenstone, *Who Votes?*, 91–93. See also Nicholas Lovrich, Jr., and Otwin Marenin, "A Comparison of Black and Mexican American Voters in Denver: Assertive vs. Acquiescent Political Orientations and Voting Behavior in an Urban Electorate," *Western Political Quarterly* 29 (1976): 284–294; F. Chris Garcia and Rudolph O. de la Garza, *The Chicano Political Experience* (North Scituate, Mass.: Duxbury Press, 1977), 94–110; and Susan MacManus and Carol Cassel, "Mexican-Americans in City Politics: Participation, Representation, and Policy Preferences," *Urban Interest* 4 (1982): 57–69.
57. Wolfinger and Rosenstone, *Who Votes?*, 93.
58. Ibid., 141.
59. Carole J. Uhlaner, Bruce E. Cain, and D. Roderick Kiewiet, "Political Participation of Ethnic Minorities in the 1980s," *Political Behavior* 11 (1989): 199, 225.
60. Ibid., 213.
61. Sandra Baxter and Marjorie Lansing, *Women and Politics*, rev. ed. (Ann Arbor:

University of Michigan Press, 1983), chap. 2. See also McGlen and O'Connor, *Women's Rights,* 99.

62. McGlen and O'Connor, *Women's Rights,* 105–106.
63. Miller and Traugott, *Sourcebook,* 310, table 5.29.
64. McGlen and O'Connor, *Women's Rights,* table 4.5.
65. Miller and Traugott, *Sourcebook,* 301, table 5.18.
66. Elise Boulding, "Familial Constraints on Women's Work Roles," in *Women and the Workplace: The Implications of Occupational Segregation,* ed. Martha Blaxall and Barbara Reagan (Chicago: University of Chicago Press, 1976), 113.
67. Miller and Traugott, *Sourcebook,* 281, table 4.46.
68. Declining differences were found in Richard M. Merelman, *Political Socialization and Educational Climates* (New York: Holt, Rinehart, and Winston, 1971); and A. Orum, R. S. Cohen, S. Grassmuck, and A. W. Orum, "Sex, Socialization, and Politics," *American Sociological Review* 39 (1974): 197–209. In contrast, Jennings and Niemi found that gender differences among a subsample of young adults increased from 1965 to 1973, even though they decreased among their parents on a number of measures of political involvement and activity: M. Kent Jennings and Richard G. Niemi, *Generations and Politics: A Panel Study of Young Adults and Their Parents* (Princeton: Princeton University Press, 1981), chap. 9.
69. Francine D. Blau, "Women in the Labor Force: An Overview," in *Women: A Feminist Perspective,* ed. Jo Freeman, 3d ed. (Palo Alto, Calif.: Mayfield, 1984), 302, table 1 and 307, table 3; and Debra Renee Kaufman, "Professional Women: How Real Are the Recent Gains"; in *Women,* ed. Freeman, 355, table 1.
70. Andersen, "Working Women," 442–443, 446–451; Kathleen McCourt, *Working Women and Grassroots Politics* (Bloomington: Indiana University Press, 1977); and Susan Welch, "Women as Political Animals? A Test of Some Explanations for Male-Female Political Participation Differences," *American Journal of Political Science* 21 (1977): 724. See also Eileen McDonagh, "To Work or Not to Work: The Differential Impact of Achieved and Derived Status upon the Political Participation of Women, 1956–1976," *American Journal of Political Science* 26 (1982): 280–297. McDonagh reports that derived status is more strongly associated with the number of campaign acts performed than is employment or achieved status based on occupational prestige measures. However, table 3 (p. 290) indicates that the pattern of relationships between the measures of employment and status and the number of campaign acts performed has varied substantially over time. Furthermore, the relationship between derived status and number of campaign acts performed may be a function of the leisure time available for campaigning.
71. Wolfinger and Rosenstone, *Who Votes?,* 43.
72. Ellen Boneparth, "Women in Campaigns: From Lickin' and Stickin' to Strategy," *American Politics Quarterly* 5 (1977): 289–300; and Albert K. Karnig and B. Oliver Walter, "Election of Women to City Councils," *Social Science Quarterly* 56 (1976): 605–613.
73. R. Darcy and Sarah Slavin Schramm, "When Women Run Against Men," *Public Opinion Quarterly* 41 (1977): 1–12; Ruth Mandel, *In the Running* (Boston: Beacon, 1981); and Jeane J. Kirkpatrick, *Political Women* (New York: Basic Books, 1974). For research that tests several alternative explanations, see Cal Clark and Janet Clark, "Models of Gender and Political Participation in the United States," *Women and Politics* 6 (1986): 5–25; Carol Christy, *Sex Differences in Political Participation* (New York: Praeger, 1987).
74. Ruy A. Teixeira, *Why Americans Don't Vote* (New York: Greenwood Press, 1987), chap. 5.

Chapter 3

The Psychology of Political
Participation

Patterns of political participation are significantly influenced by the psychological orientations of citizens. Among these orientations are attitudes, beliefs, and values, all of which change, as do their relationships to political participation. Also relevant to an understanding of political participation is the study of personality, especially of the motives underlying the performance of certain kinds of political actions and the characteristic behavior patterns of politicians who have certain types of personalities.

Attitudes, Beliefs, and Values

Beliefs can be classified into three different types: (1) *descriptive,* a person's perception of the way things are (for example, "the U.S. Congress has 535 voting members"); (2) *evaluative,* a person's judgment of people or events ("Franklin Roosevelt was a very skilled political leader"); and (3) *prescriptive,* a person's view of preferred courses of action or modes of behavior ("nuclear war should be avoided"). Beliefs have several components—cognitive (knowledge), affective (emotion-arousing), and behavioral (action-stimulating). Each belief is a predisposition that, when activated, leads toward some preferential response.

An *attitude* is a "relatively enduring organization of interrelated beliefs that describe, evaluate, and advocate with respect to an object or situation."[1] Attitudes may focus on either objects (including people) or situations, and both are important in influencing political participation. For example, objects such as presidential candidates will be evaluated by citizens in terms of how they might perform in different situations (setting budget priorities, managing routine foreign policy activities, handling an international crisis). Prospective evaluations of how each object (candidate) would react in different situations may be instrumental in deciding whether and how to vote.[2]

In contrast to attitudes and beliefs, values are statements of "goods," situations or objects that are preferred to other situations or objects. Values can be categorized as *terminal* or *instrumental*. Instrumental values are ideal forms of behavior, such as affectionate, intellectual, and imaginative, while terminal values are idealized end states, such as equality, justice, freedom, peace, and happiness.[3] Terminal values can in turn be divided into material and nonmaterial ones.[4]

Trends in Psychological Involvement in Politics

Psychological involvement refers to the possession of a complex structure of attitudes, beliefs, and values with respect to some object. It is a plausible expectation that those who have a greater psychological involvement in politics will be more active politically. Among the components of psychological involvement in politics are a perceived obligation to participate (civic duty), interest in politics, interest in a current or impending political campaign, sense of personal political effectiveness (political efficacy), and identification with a political party.[5]

Holding higher levels of these attitudes tends to stimulate more political activism. For example, a study of individuals registered to vote in ten elections held over several years in one state indicated that the levels of interest in politics, partisan identification, perception of party differences, and sense of civic obligation were related to the frequency with which individuals voted in those elections.[6]

The strength of the belief that an individual has an obligation or duty to participate in politics showed little change between 1956 and 1980. Between 45 and 49 percent of survey respondents indicated a high level of civic duty and 13 to 15 percent a

TABLE 3-1
Level of Belief in Civic Duty, 1952–1980
(percent of respondents at each level)

	1952	1956	1960	1972	1976	1978	1980
Low	17	13	10	14	14	15	14
Middle	40	37	37	36	36	36	33
High	40	48	49	49	48	45	48
Not scored	3	2	3	2	3	3	5

SOURCES: Data for 1952–1978 from Warren E. Miller, Arthur H. Miller, and Edward J. Schneider, *American National Election Studies Data Sourcebook, 1952–1978* (Cambridge: Harvard University Press, 1980), 288, table 4.43. Copyright © 1980 by the President and Fellows of Harvard College; used by permission. Data for 1980 from the American National Election Study, Center for Political Studies, University of Michigan.

Note: The index of level of belief in civic duty was constructed from respondents' degree of agreement with four statements: (1) Sometimes so many other people vote in the national elections that it doesn't matter much whether you vote or not. (2) If you don't care how an election comes out, you shouldn't vote in it. (3) It isn't so important to vote when you know your party doesn't have a chance to win. (4) A good many local elections aren't important enough to bother with. The full set of statements was not included in the survey after 1980.

low level (see Table 3-1). The level of general interest in politics has changed, but not in a monotonic fashion (see Table 3-2). Interest appears to have risen to a peak during the tumultuous decade spanning the last half of the 1960s and first half of the 1970s, when the civil rights movement, the Vietnam War, the Watergate scandal with the subsequent resignation of President Nixon and his pardon by President Ford, the recession of 1973–1974, and the first major energy crisis inflamed public passions. As these issues decreased in importance to the electorate during the late 1970s, political interest declined correspondingly. The level of interest in the current campaign, however, has been more stable; since 1952, between 30 and 39 percent of the voters have said they were "very much" interested in it. Interest in the congressional campaigns in the midterm years has been more variable but consistently lower (see Table 3-3).

Another component of psychological involvement in politics is one's sense of internal and external political efficacy. The proportion of survey respondents rated as having a low level of internal political efficacy—the belief that one can understand politics and government and that political events can be influenced by the activities of individuals like oneself—ranged from

TABLE 3-2

Level of General Interest in Politics, 1960–1988

(percent giving each response)

	1960	1962	1964	1966	1968	1972	1974	1976	1978	1980	1982	1984	1986	1988
Hardly at all	38	42	11	17	18	11	11	12	17	16	15	14	15	15
Only now and then	—	—	17	18	19	16	14	18	25	23	21	23	24	25
Some of the time	42	43	42	30	31	36	36	31	34	35	35	36	35	37
Most of the time	21	16	30	35	33	37	39	38	23	26	29	26	26	22
Don't know	0	0	0	0	0	0	1	1	1	0	0	0	0	0

SOURCE: American National Election Studies, Center for Political Studies, University of Michigan.

Note: Figures are based on responses to the following question: "Some people seem to follow what's going on in government and public affairs most of the time, whether there's an election going on or not. Others aren't that interested. Would you say that you follow what's going on in government and public affairs most of the time, some of the time, only now and then, or hardly at all?" The response alternative "only now and then" was not used in 1960 and 1962.

TABLE 3-3
Level of Interest in the Current Political Campaign, 1952–1988
(percent indicating each level of interest)

	Presidential campaigns									
	1952	1956	1960	1964	1968	1972	1976	1980	1984	1988
Not much	29	31	25	25	21	27	21	26	20	22
Somewhat	34	40	37	37	40	41	42	44	45	46
Very much	37	30	38	38	39	32	37	30	35	31

	Midterm congressional campaigns							
	1958	1962	1966	1970	1974	1978	1982	1986
Not much	41	26	30	24	—	34	30	22
Somewhat	33	38	40	43	—	45	44	44
Very much	27	36	30	34	—	22	26	33

SOURCE: American National Election Studies, Center for Political Studies, University of Michigan.

Note: Figures are based on responses to the following question: "Some people don't pay much attention to the political campaigns. How about you? Would you say that you have been/were very much interested, somewhat interested, or not much interested in the political campaign (so far) this year?"

57 percent to 47 percent between 1952 and 1980, while 6 to 18 percent of the electorate were rated as having a high level, with no noticeable trend in either direction (Table 3-4). The proportion with high external political efficacy—the belief that public officials are responsive to the interests of individuals like oneself and that governmental and political institutions help make them responsive—has declined significantly during the same period (Table 3-5).

Strength of identification with a political party, another dimension of psychological involvement in politics, has been measured since 1952 with the same set of questions. Respondents are initially asked, "Generally speaking, do you usually think of yourself as a Republican, a Democrat, or an Independent, or what?" Those responding "Democrat" or "Republican" are asked, "Would you call yourself a strong Republican (Democrat) or a not very strong Republican (Democrat)?" Those responding "Independent" are asked, "Do you think of yourself as closer to the Republican or the Democratic party?" From these questions a seven-point scale of partisan identification is created, ranging

TABLE 3-4

Level of Internal Political Efficacy, 1952–1980

(percent of respondents at each level)

	1952	1956	1960	1964	1968	1970	1972	1974	1976	1978	1980
Low	58	50	46	55	47	49	51	50	55	48	47
Medium	29	36	38	32	33	34	34	35	31	36	39
High	7	12	13	11	18	16	15	14	13	15	14
Not scored	7	1	3	1	2	1	1	1	1	1	0

SOURCE: American National Election Studies, Center for Political Studies, University of Michigan.

Note: Level of internal political efficacy was measured by the responses to two items: "Voting is the only way that people like me can have a say about how the government runs things" and "Sometimes politics and government seem so complicated that a person like me can't really understand what's going on." Persons who disagreed with both these items were scored "high"; those who disagreed with one were scored "medium"; and those who did not disagree with either were scored "low." The full set of items is not available in data sets collected after 1980.

from "Strong Democrat" to "Strong Republican," with "Independent" in the middle. The proportion of respondents who call themselves independent has been increasing since the measure was first taken, with corresponding decreases in the proportion who identify strongly with either party (Table 3-6).

Blacks have been more Democratic than whites during the last three decades; this reflects their perceptions of the policies promoted and enacted by Democratic presidents and Democratic-controlled Congresses. The proportion of whites claiming to be strong Democrats dropped from 32 percent in 1952 to 28 percent in 1982 and to 16 percent by 1988 in the South. Outside the South, the proportion of whites who identified strongly with the Democratic party dropped from a high of 24 percent in 1964 to 17 percent in 1982 and to 13 percent in 1988. In both regions, the proportion of the electorate reporting themselves to be either independents who are closer to one party or independents who divide their voting support between the two parties increased. Among blacks, on the other hand, the proportion of strong identifiers remained high until 1972, when it began to decline.

Between 1952 and 1984, the proportion of blacks who were strong Republican party identifiers decreased, but the trend began to reverse in 1986, with the proportion of blacks who iden-

TABLE 3-5

Level of External Political Efficacy, 1952–1988
(percent of respondents at each level)

	1952	1956	1960	1964	1968	1970	1972	1974	1976	1978	1980	1984	1988
Low	20	17	15	22	30	26	32	32	45	35	32	24	43
Medium	25	22	22	27	24	33	28	32	24	31	34	24	27
High	48	59	60	50	43	40	40	35	30	33	34	49	30
Not scored	8	1	3	1	4	0	1	1	1	1	1	3	—

SOURCE: American National Election Studies, Center for Political Studies, University of Michigan.

Note: Level of external political efficacy was measured by the responses to two items: "People like me don't have any say about what the government does," and "I don't think public officials care much about what people like me think." Persons who disagreed with both these items were scored "high"; those who disagreed with one were scored "medium"; and those who did not disagree with either were scored "low."

TABLE 3-6

Party Identification, 1952–1988

(percent reporting each type of identification)

	1952	1954	1956	1958	1960	1962	1964	1966	1968	1970	1972	1974	1976	1978	1980	1982	1984	1986	1988
Strong Democrat	22	22	21	27	20	23	27	18	20	20	15	18	15	15	18	20	18	18	18
Weak Democrat	25	26	23	22	25	23	25	28	25	24	26	21	25	24	23	24	22	22	18
Independent-leaning Democrat	10	9	6	7	6	7	9	9	10	10	11	13	12	14	11	11	10	10	12
Independent	6	7	9	7	10	8	8	12	11	13	13	15	15	14	13	11	6	12	11
Independent-leaning Republican	7	6	8	5	7	6	6	7	9	8	11	9	10	10	10	8	13	11	13
Weak Republican	14	14	14	17	14	16	14	15	15	15	13	14	14	13	14	14	15	15	14
Strong Republican	14	13	15	11	16	12	11	10	10	9	10	8	9	8	9	10	14	10	14
Apolitical	3	4	4	4	3	4	1	1	1	1	1	3	1	3	2	2	2	2	0

SOURCE: American National Election Studies, Center for Political Studies, University of Michigan.
Note: For method of determining identification, see text.

tify strongly with the Republican party increasing slightly in the South, but not in the North.

Several other changes are evident in patterns of party identification. Citizens coming of voting age since World War II are less likely to be strong Democrats and more likely to be either independents who usually support one party or pure independents than are older citizens, and the proportion of independents is greatest among the most recent entrants into the electorate.[7] In contrast, older age groups were more likely to be strong Democrats during the 1980s than they were in the 1960s and 1970s. The decline in partisanship among younger cohorts began in the mid-1960s and occurred among both the high-school-educated and college-educated (an increasingly large proportion of the electorate), but not among those with only a grade school education.[8]

In summary, a significant decline has taken place in two of the components of psychological involvement: Fewer citizens have a partisan identification, and the sense of external political efficacy has decreased among a significant proportion of the electorate.

Trends in Other Attitudes and Beliefs

While external political efficacy measures citizens' perceptions of government's responsiveness to people like themselves, another measure—government attentiveness—taps citizens' perceptions of the responsiveness of Congress and of political leaders to the wishes of the general public and the effectiveness of elections and political parties in facilitating that responsiveness. This measure shows a substantial decline since 1964. The proportion scoring in the two highest categories has dropped from 61 percent in 1964 to 38 percent in 1980, the most recent year for which the measure is available (Table 3-7).

Citizens' responses to the question, "How much of the time do you think you can trust the government in Washington to do what is right—just about always, most of the time, or only some of the time?" changed substantially from 1958 to 1988. The proportion responding "most of the time" or "just about al-

TABLE 3-7

Level of Belief in Government Attentiveness, 1964–1980

(percent scored at each level)

	1964	1968	1970	1972	1974	1976	1978	1980
Low	5	8	8	6	8	10	8	11
	12	15	19	19	24	24	19	26
↓	16	18	16	23	22	19	21	19
	29	29	32	33	30	34	33	32
High	32	25	22	17	12	9	11	6
Not scored	5	5	4	3	4	3	9	6

SOURCES: Data for 1964–1978 from Warren E. Miller, Arthur H. Miller, and Edward J. Schneider, *American National Election Studies Data Sourcebook, 1952–1978* (Cambridge: Harvard University Press, 1980), 283, table 4.40. Copyright © 1980 by the President and Fellows of Harvard College; used by permission. Data for 1980 from the American National Election Study, Center for Political Studies, University of Michigan.

Note: Figures are based on responses to the following questions: (1) "Over the years, how much attention do you feel the government pays to what people think when it decides what to do?" (2) "Do you feel that political parties help to make the government pay attention to what the people think?" (3) "Do you feel that having elections makes the government pay attention to what the people think?" (4) "How much attention do you think most congressmen pay to the people who elect them when they decide what to do in Congress?" The full set of items was not included in the election surveys after 1980.

ways" reached 76 percent in 1964, but declined to 37 percent in 1974, reflecting reactions to the Vietnam War, domestic policy changes, and the Watergate scandal. The decline continued through 1980, with the proportion of the electorate giving a more trusting response reaching a low of 25 percent. A revival of trust began during the Reagan administration, with 35 percent giving a more trusting response by 1988.[9]

Aside from these short-term variations, Huntington has argued that during certain periods of American history, the gap between the ideals of the American political system and the actual performance of its institutions and leaders becomes too large to be tolerated by a substantial number of citizens. This gap stimulates heightened levels of distrust of political leaders, demands for changes in the structures and operations of political institutions, and increased levels of political activity.[10]

While higher levels of interest in a campaign can stimulate political participation, individuals are more likely to participate in an election if they also care about who wins it. That concern may focus on the outcome of a highly visible and nationally important contest, such as that for the presidency. On the other hand, in a city such as Chicago, with a tradition of a strong party organization and party influence in the distribution of patronage jobs and neighborhood services, citizens may feel deep concern over the outcomes of mayoral and city council elections and even local political-party committee offices. A number of national surveys have asked citizens how much they personally care about which party wins the presidential election or, in midterm years, the congressional elections. About two-thirds of those surveyed between 1952 and 1968 indicated they cared "a good deal" about the outcome of the presidential election, but the proportion declined steadily thereafter, standing at only 44 percent in 1980. However, the proportion expressing a good deal of concern with presidential election outcomes rebounded in 1984 and 1988 (Table 3-8). The proportion expressing "a good deal" of concern about the outcome of congressional elections has shown a similar trend.

Effect of Attitudes and Beliefs on Political Participation

The attitudes and beliefs that have been discussed vary in their relationship to political participation. General interest in politics, interest in the campaign, and sense of civic duty have maintained a stable, though moderate, relationship with voter turnout during the past thirty years. Trust in government has also had a stable association with voter turnout, but it has been a weaker one. Those who are low in trust in government are about as likely to vote as are those who are high in trust.[11] Those who identify strongly with a party have generally been more likely to vote (and to participate in other ways) than those who do not.[12]

The patterns of relationships between other measures of psychological involvement and voter turnout have not remained stable. Internal efficacy has had a curvilinear relationship, remaining relatively stable from 1952 to 1960, dropping between 1960 and 1964, then slowly increasing again. The effect of internal efficacy can be described as weak to moderate; those having higher levels of internal efficacy are at best moderately more likely to vote. In 1976, for example, 62 percent of those with the lowest level of

TABLE 3-8
Level of Concern over Which Party Wins Election,
1952–1988
(percent giving response indicated)

	Don't care or don't know	Care a good deal
1952	33	67
1956	37	63
1958	47	53
1960	35	65
1964	35	66
1968	35	65
1970	35	65
1972	40	60
1974	43	57
1976	43	57
1978	57	43
1980	56	44
1984	34	66
1988	39	61

SOURCE: American National Election Studies, Center for Political Studies, University of Michigan.

Note: Figures represent responses to the following question: "Generally speaking, would you say that you personally care/cared a good deal which party wins/won the presidential election (elections to the Congress in Washington) this fall, or don't you care which party wins/won?" The question was not asked in 1954, 1962, or 1966. In 1982, a different set of response categories was used, with these results: care "very much," 21 percent; "pretty much," 37 percent; "not very much," 30 percent; and "not at all," 12 percent.

internal efficacy reported having voted, compared to 90 percent of those with the highest level of internal efficacy.[13] Both internal and external efficacy are also moderately associated with turnout in presidential elections, but they are only weakly associated with turnout in midterm elections. The strength of the relationships declined slightly between 1968 and 1972, then stabilized.[14] The relationship between believing the government to be responsive and voter turnout has been generally low, but it increased slightly from 1964 to 1974 and then began a decline that has continued since that time.[15]

Perception of the closeness of the presidential election (Table 3-9) has had the widest variation in effects on electoral activities. During the era of political turmoil from 1964 to 1972, perceived closeness had little impact on participation: Those who expected it to be close were no more likely to participate than were those who expected it to be a landslide. Other factors, especially the level of satisfaction with the economic, social, and foreign policies of the time, were clearly more important. If the level of dissatisfaction is sufficiently large, citizens will engage in electoral activity regardless of their perceptions of the closeness of the outcome. Furthermore, other contests, such as those for the Senate and House of Representatives, can also serve as a vehicle for expressions of policy discontent. Before 1964 and after 1972, however, perceived closeness did have a moderate effect, with those expecting it to be close participating somewhat more (Table 3-9).

One set of citizens' beliefs relevant to the explanation of patterns of political behavior is beliefs about the utility or futility of traditional forms of political participation in making the government responsive to citizens' views. A series of questions have been included in the biennial National Election Studies surveys to examine these beliefs. The general trend from 1964 to 1980 was an increased perception of the government as not responsive to citizens' views. Both the government in general and the Congress were not believed to be very attentive to citizens' preferences. Parties are not perceived as an effective mechanism to force government attentiveness to citizens' views and are also

TABLE 3-9
Expected Closeness of Presidential Election, 1952–1988
(percent giving each response)

	1952	1956	1960	1964	1968	1972	1976	1980	1984	1988
Will win by quite a bit	20	25	12	43	20	56	14	15	46	25
Will be a close race	61	57	64	42	60	32	70	79	48	69
Don't know	19	18	25	16	20	13	17	6	6	5
Correlation coefficient (gamma) with index of political participation	.10	.14	.23	−.02	.03	−.03	.13	.05	.05	.07

SOURCE: American National Election Studies, Center for Political Studies, University of Michigan.
Note: Figures are based on responses to the following question: "Do you think it will be a close race or will [respondent's predicted winning candidate] win by quite a bit?"

perceived as interested simply in obtaining votes, not in reflecting citizens' opinions. However, a majority of those surveyed still believe elections to be an effective mechanism to force government attentiveness to citizen preferences.

Participation can be affected by a citizen's calculations of its likely benefits. According to one theory, each citizen estimates the benefits likely to be derived from different policy outcomes and also takes into account the personal costs of attempting to influence these outcomes. Another variable in the calculation is the relative probability that different outcomes will result from varying levels of effort.[16] For example, an individual may conclude that a senatorial election is going to result in a landslide victory for the incumbent, and that the probability of his or her vote influencing the outcome of the Senate contest is so small that casting a vote is not worth the effort. In contrast, where an election appears to be very closely contested, citizens may be more motivated to participate, believing that their votes and campaign activities may have an impact on the outcome. As Table 3-9 indicates, presidential elections do vary considerably in the extent to which they are perceived as being close contests.

In 1960 and 1968, the presidential elections resulted in narrow victories in terms of popular votes. Only two-tenths of a percentage point separated the popular vote for the Democratic and Republican candidates in 1960, and voter turnout in that election was the highest in modern times, with 60 percent of those eligible casting ballots. In 1968, Republican candidate Richard M. Nixon received 43.4 percent and Democratic candidate Hubert H. Humphrey received 42.7 percent of the popular votes cast; voter turnout was slightly lower than in the preceding election but more than 5 percent higher than it would be in the next.

As for the effect of values on participation, a study of young citizens in five nations presents some evidence that those who seek material goals are less likely to be politically active than are those who are more concerned with the quality of life.[17]

The Acquisition of Political Orientations

Attitudes, beliefs, and values are learned predispositions, and the various forms of political participation are learned behavior. The legal structure and other elements of the political and social environment create a context within which attitudes, beliefs, and values are used and behaviors (a political-action "repertory") are put into effect. However, behaviors can be learned but not used. For example, children learn to throw balls, rocks, and other objects, but that does not mean that as adults they will necessarily engage in rock-throwing demonstrations when political leaders implement policies with which they strongly disagree.

Studies of the learning of political orientations and behaviors provide some answers to questions about who engages in what forms of political action. Political education begins in early childhood, when children learn attitudes, beliefs, and values primarily through overhearing the conversations of family members about political objects and events. Family discussions about public officials, such as a president, governor, mayor, police officer, or bureaucrat in a governmental agency, create images of public authorities and of the political regime. Occasionally a family may try to inculcate particular political attitudes through discussions deliberately aimed at both adding to a child's knowledge and fostering certain attitudes and beliefs.[18]

While the family remains an important source of political education, the widespread availability of television network news since the late 1950s and early 1960s has undoubtedly increased the importance of the mass media as instruments of political learning for both children and adults. Learning through television occurs best with frequent repetition; complex ideas may not be easily acquired through a passive learning mechanism such as television, but both beliefs and attitudes can be acquired or reinforced through the mass media.[19] By showing individuals engaging in both conventional and unconventional forms of political behavior and political leaders' responses to these acts, the mass media help individuals learn about such forms of political activity and assess their effectiveness in obtaining desired results. Through choosing to emphasize some problems and not others, the mass media also help establish the public-policy agenda.

Some scholars have argued that television has contributed to lower levels of political participation. Studies of television news coverage of elections conclude that it fosters a general bias against all major candidates while ignoring minor candidates. The image conveyed by television news is of a set of independent political entrepreneurs playing games in order to win particular political offices. The importance of policy differences between candidates and the role of institutions such as the political parties are ignored. In effect, television creates an image of politics as a horse race and fosters a set of negative attitudes toward politics and toward participation in politics.[20] It was noted earlier that among the major trends in political attitudes during the past two decades is a decline in partisan attachments, trust in government, and external political efficacy. That these declines occurred during the rise of television as a major source of political information is probably not a coincidence.

Friends and acquaintances can also play a significant role in children's political socialization. For example, adolescents whose friends hold political attitudes congruent with parental attitudes are even more likely to have attitudes similar to their parents. Children whose parents' attitudes are dissimilar to those predominant in the community are more likely to adopt attitudes different from their parents and similar to those dominant in the community.[21]

While childhood socialization plays an important role in the acquisition of political orientations and the learning of forms of political action, political learning is lifelong. As life experiences change, so also do political orientations. A study of high-school students and their parents, who were first interviewed in 1965 and then again in 1973, found that changes in political attitudes, beliefs, and behavior occurred among both the parents and the children, following upon changes in their personal circumstances and political conditions.[22]

Engaging in political action influences subsequent attitudes and behavior. For example, participation in elections through either voting or engaging in campaign activities has a positive effect on citizens' later sense of political efficacy.[23] Participation in protest demonstrations also has a socializing effect on other attitudes. Those who participated in protest demonstrations while college students during the Vietnam War were later more likely to be supportive of civil liberties, to oppose prayer in schools, and to support racial integration in schools than were those who had not protested. However, the protesters became significantly less liberal on most issues as they grew older, with the exception of one issue—support for women's equality.[24]

Political learning can be direct or indirect. Indirect political learning is the acquisition of psychological orientations that are politically relevant even though they are not explicitly political.[25] For example, an individual might transfer attitudes toward parental and school authorities to political authorities.[26] Another form of indirect learning is apprenticeship. Skills such as public speaking, organizing ability, and running meetings may be learned in other realms but transferred to political arenas. By participating in social organizations with hierarchical structures and formal rules, people learn to operate within organizational frameworks, and this pattern of behavior can be generalized to the political system.[27]

Direct political learning can be accomplished through imitating the political views and actions of others—for example, adopting the political-party identification of one's parents. Direct learning can be anticipatory, as when individuals set out to learn the orientations and skills needed to fill a political role, such as candidate for public office. Direct learning can also occur through experience; for example, attitudes toward government authorities can be significantly altered by dealings with public officials, such as a police officer or a clerk at the state motor vehicle administration office.[28]

Another vehicle of political learning is the educational system. Formal schooling acts to inculcate political beliefs, attitudes, and values and to instill forms of political behavior in students in a number of ways:

The school accomplishes political socialization through its curriculum, classroom rituals, and values, and attitudes unconsciously transmitted by its staff. The school's social climate, political and non-political organizations, and extracurricular activities exert subtle socializing influences. The effects of being educated about political affairs, also a task of the school, bear on political socialization.[29]

Personality and Political Participation

Personality can be defined as "the pattern of traits characterizing an individual person, trait here meaning any psychological characteristic of a person, including dispositions to perceive different situations similarly and to react consistently despite changing stimulus conditions, values, abilities, motives, defenses and aspects of temperament, identity, and personal style."[30] What we call personality is basically a set of inferences that we make about individuals on the basis of a set of concepts. The set of concepts depends upon which particular variety of personality theory we use (for example, Freudian, Jungian, Maslovian). If we assume that political action is the consequence not only of the environment in which individuals are located but also of the psychological predispositions they bring to the situation, then knowledge of personality characteristics can help account for both the level and the type of such action.

A number of approaches exist to the study of personality, but the ideas of motive and control are basic to all of them. One example of a theory of motivation that can be used to explain patterns of political participation is Maslow's needs theory. Maslow suggests a hierarchy of five basic types of needs that stimulate human behavior: physical (for example, food, water, shelter); security; affection, love, and belongingness; self-esteem; and self-actualization.[31]

The first need of individuals, according to Maslow, is the basic necessities of life—food and shelter. In developed democracies governments are expected to provide these to citizens, and many programs at the level of local, state, and national government are designed to provide them. Demands presented through various types of political acts focus on such issues as the adequacy of programs—for example, the quantity and quality of food provided through food stamps and surplus food programs—or the extent of the programs, such as the proportion of the homeless served by shelter programs.

Maslow places security second in his list of human needs. The absence of security in the natural order of relationships among human beings was seen by the political philosopher Thomas Hobbes as the stimulus for the formation of governments.[32] One factor contributing to the perception of a government as legitimate is its ability to provide citizens with security of person and property. The failure of a government to provide food, shelter, and security to some portion of the citizenry can lead to demands for government programs made in both traditional and nontraditional forms of political action.

Maslow lists the need to be loved and to belong to a group as third in his hierarchy. Research suggests that persons relatively isolated from society are more likely to support extremist political movements.[33] Psychological profiles of political assassins also suggest that they are frequently socially isolated individuals.[34]

It can also be hypothesized that those who participate in forms of political activity other than voting, such as working in political organizations, seek to satisfy a basic need for belongingness. For example, considerable research suggests that political-party activists who initially became involved for other reasons, such as concern with a particular issue or support for a candidate, report a major current satisfaction to be the social rewards of their involvement, such as group camaraderie and enjoyment of the social contacts.[35]

The fourth need suggested by Maslow is the need for self-esteem or self-respect. If social norms emphasize that individuals should participate in a certain way, such as voting, then individuals' self-respect requirements would act as a stimulus for voting participation. Some researchers have argued that political elites may be motivated by a need for self-esteem; while politics is only one avenue for obtaining heightened self-esteem, it is one that can bring considerable psychic rewards to the individual.[36] If the drive for equality can be considered a component of the search for self-esteem, that need can be viewed as a stimulus to participation in the women's movement and the civil rights movement in the United States and in various anticolonial movements in many parts of the world during the twentieth century.

The fifth need in Maslow's hierarchy is self-actualization—the need to develop personal capabilities and pursue interests to the fullest extent possible. The Declaration of Independence held the pursuit of happiness to be an "unalienable right" and its absence a justification for the American colonies' revolt against Great Britain. Those who perceive the government to be unduly inhibiting of their pursuit of happiness may take action against government policies, leaders, and institutions through demonstrations, protests, and even—as in the case just cited—armed rebellions. On the other hand, some government programs and activities can be viewed as mechanisms for enabling individuals to obtain self-actualization; in the modern context, these might include, for example, loans and grants to students to finance their college education.

Advocates of participatory democracy argue that the act of participation itself contributes to individuals' self-actualization and that therefore participatory decision-making processes should be used to the greatest extent possible. In this view, not only would the quality of decisions be improved when more individuals are actively involved in the process, but also the individuals participating would be better persons and better citizens as a consequence of their participation. In other words, human growth and development—that is, self-actualization—is stimulated through involvement in politics and in governmental decision making.[37] Individuals acquire knowledge and develop more positive attitudes toward themselves, the community, and the larger society, thereby reducing negative attitudes such as political cynicism and mistrust and increasing the legitimacy accorded the political system and its institutions, leaders, and policies.[38]

Theories of personality other than Maslow's emphasize different types of needs. For example, McClelland specifies three basic needs: power, achievement, and affiliation.[39] One application of this theory to the study of political recruitment suggests that individuals with different types of need patterns are recruited by different methods and behave differently in political office.[40] (Of course, individuals must learn that they can satisfy various needs through political activity if these needs are to lead them toward political participation.) Research indicates that individuals with high affiliation needs tend to be recruited to run for office by others, rather than being self-recruited. After obtaining public office, behavior in office also varies with patterns of needs, with individuals who have a high need for power tending to focus on organizational maintenance and control while those who have a high need for achievement tend to emphasize policy concerns rather than organizational influence. Individuals who have a continuing commitment to work toward obtaining certain policy goals are high in both need for achievement and need for power.[41]

Personality theory has also been used to develop typologies of the behavior of various types of political actors, such as executives or legislators. One study presents a scheme of presidential types, in which a president's style, world view, and character create personality patterns, which are then viewed as interacting with the distribution of political power to create expectations about how the president will behave, and all of these together are seen as determining how presidents carry out their obligations.[42] In this theory, presidential character is defined along two dimensions. One is energy level; both Lyndon Johnson and John Kennedy would be described as "active" types, while Calvin Coolidge was a "passive" type. The second dimension is affect, or the president's attitude toward his activity. Both Theodore Roosevelt and Franklin Roosevelt enjoyed being president, but other presidents, such as Woodrow Wilson, were negative toward their job, viewing it as a great burden. This leads to a fourfold typology: active-positive (Roosevelt, Truman, Kennedy); active-negative (Hoover, Wilson, Lyndon Johnson, Nixon); passive-positive (Taft, Harding); and passive-negative (Coolidge).[43] Thus, personality theories may be useful in understanding both who is recruited to participate in various types of political roles and how various individuals perform in these political roles.

Psychological Influences on
Unconventional Forms of Participation

During the tumultuous period from 1960 through the early 1970s, public attitudes in the United States became more supportive of the use of nonconventional means of expressing dissatisfaction with public policies and making demands for changes. Approval of participation in protests or demonstrations permitted by local authorities increased slightly, reaching a high of 18 percent in 1972, the high point of public protest against the Vietnam War, but disapproval of protest participation dropped from 49 percent to 40 percent. Approval of refusing to obey a law the individual considers to be unjust also increased during this period, rising to 16 percent in 1972, although it then declined to only 6 percent by 1976. However, the percent disapproving of disobedience under any conditions dropped from 52 percent in 1970 to 29 percent in 1976, with a concomitant increase in the proportion saying that whether individuals should refuse to obey an unjust law would depend on the circumstances. Approval of stopping government activity by means of such actions as sit-ins, mass meetings, and demonstrations increased slightly, rising to 8 percent by 1974, while the proportion disapproving of such activity dropped to 51 percent in 1974 from 63 percent in 1970.[44]

A study in 1974 of citizens in five different countries examined their approval of ten different types of unconventional political action. In the United States, a majority approved of signing petitions, engaging in lawful demonstrations, and participating in boycotts, but only a minority approved of each of the other seven forms of behavior, with personal violence, the least favored form, receiving the approval of only 2 percent of those surveyed. Only for petition signing did a majority (58 percent) report that they themselves had engaged in the activity, while another 20 percent indicated that they would be willing to sign petitions. Only 11 percent reported having engaged in lawful demonstrations, and 28 percent reported that they would do so under some conditions. Participation in boycotts was reported by 15 percent, while another 20 percent responded that they would participate in certain circumstances. In the other four nations a majority approved only of signing petitions and lawful demonstrations but fewer people had actually engaged in these activities than had done so in the United States.[45]

Of those surveyed in the United States, 80 percent thought that petitions were effective in obtaining political changes, and two-thirds credited lawful demonstrations and boycotts with effectiveness. No other form of unconventional behavior was assessed as effective by as much as 40 percent of the sample, with 11 percent evaluating personal violence as effective.[46] Support for unconventional forms of political action increased substantially in the United States and several European nations during the past two decades,[47] with various forms of protest activity more likely to be engaged in by younger citizens and by those with lower levels of education.[48]

Some beliefs, attitudes, and values contribute to participation in unconventional political behavior.[49] Participation is conditioned by beliefs about peer and community approval or disapproval of that form of political activity, positive or negative attitudes toward it, and assessments of the extent to which it is effective in achieving the desired ends.[50] Various forms of political protest are also more likely to be supported by individuals who place greater emphasis on nonmaterialistic values and who tend to think about politics in ideological terms more than in terms of the nature of the times or political personalities.[51]

Alienation and Conformism

One explanation that has been offered for nonparticipation in American politics is that those who do not participate are "alienated" from the political system. As an objective condition, alienation is the absence of social norms as perceived by observers of a society; as a subjective condition, it is a feeling of discrepancy between expectations and reality held by an individual or set of individuals.[52] Finifter has delineated four ways in which political alienation may be expressed: (1) *political powerlessness,* defined as the feeling of inability to affect the actions of the government—in effect, a low sense of political efficacy; (2) *political meaninglessness,* reflecting a view of political events as unpredictable and unpatterned; (3) *normlessness,* the perception that societal norms are not being followed and the traditional social and political order has broken down; and (4) *political isolation,* the belief that no legitimate norms governing the political system exist.[53]

In a study of alienation as a subjective condition among younger citizens, Keniston described it as having four dimensions:

1. *Focus*—From what is the individual alienated?
2. *Replacement*—What replaces the previous relationship?
3. *Mode*—How is the alienation manifested?
4. *Agent*—What is the agent of alienation?[54]

These four dimensions can be variously combined, resulting in a large number of types of alienation.[55] In Keniston's schema, alienation is contrasted with conformism. Whereas the alienated person rejects behavioral norms and cultural values, the conformist accepts them. Keniston emphasizes two foci of alienation—behavioral norms and cultural values. Behavioral norms are defined as "the common social expectations about the kind of behavior that is proper, appropriate, and legal in any society," and cultural values refer to "general conceptions of the desirable."[56] Such values might include achievement, progress, and peace. He also emphasizes two modes of expression. One is an attempt to change the world (alloplastic mode); the other is an attempt to change oneself (autoplastic mode). Alienation may be expressed through such diverse forms of behavior as terrorism, sedition, agitation, civil disobedience, social criticism, self-isolation, and delinquency or crime. Those who are alienated may withdraw, or they may become politically active, engaging in many different types of political action. Such activities as vigilantism, legalism, patriotic acts, ritualism, and compliance can be forms of expression for conformism.

This approach implies that a tendency toward alienation or conformism, in combination with personality variables, influences the individual's political behavior. David Schwartz argues further that these attitudes interact with situational variables, such as media content, group orientations, and other aspects of the individual's political environment, to produce patterns of political behavior.[57] Keniston's approach accounts for the wide range of behaviors that can result from the interaction of attitudes, environmental stimuli, and environmental constraints.

Summary

Several aspects of citizens' psychological characteristics can affect who participates in politics and the extent to which they participate. Individuals vary in both the relative importance of different motives and the extent to which they seek to satisfy different motives through political action. A number of different theories of personality, with different conceptualizations of human motivation, have been developed by psychologists and can be used in explaining patterns of political action.

Another set of factors can be grouped under the label of "psychological involvement." The higher the level of psychological involvement, the greater the expected number and variety of political acts in which citizens will engage. During the past two decades, some components of psychological involvement have declined among American citizens, resulting in a decrease in levels of political participation of the conventional type. Citizens' trust in political leaders has declined, and cynicism has increased. Some research suggests that value patterns influence types of political participation, with those who hold nonmaterialistic values tending to engage in its unconventional forms.

Parents, peers, the educational system, the mass media, and government officials all contribute to the formation of beliefs about and attitudes toward the political system. The learning of politically relevant attitudes, beliefs, values, and behaviors can occur through both direct and indirect processes of political socialization.

NOTES

1. M. Margaret Conway and Frank B. Feigert, *Political Analysis*, 2d ed. (Boston: Allyn and Bacon, 1976), 130.
2. Warren E. Miller and Merrill Shanks, "Policy Direction and Presidential Leadership: Alternative Interpretations of the 1980 Presidential Election," *British Journal of Political Science* 12 (1982): 299–356.

3. Milton Rokeach, *The Nature of Human Values* (New York: Free Press, 1973), 5–11.

4. Ronald Inglehart, *The Silent Revolution* (Princeton: Princeton University Press, 1977).

5. See, for example, Richard Brody, "The Puzzle of Political Participation," in *The New American Political System,* ed. A. King (Washington, D.C.: American Enterprise Institute, 1978), 287–324.

6. Lee Sigelman, Philip Roeder, Malcolm Jewell, and Michael Baer, "Voting and Non-Voting: A Multi-Election Perspective," *American Journal of Political Science* 29 (November 1985): 749–765.

7. Warren E. Miller and Santa Traugott, *American National Election Studies Data Sourcebook 1952–1986* (Cambridge: Harvard University Press, 1989), 82, table 2.2.

8. Ibid., 82, table 2.2.

9. Ibid., 261, table 4.12.

10. Samuel Huntington, *American Politics: The Promise of Disharmony* (Cambridge: Belknap Press, Harvard University Press, 1981).

11. Miller and Traugott, *Sourcebook,* 307, table 5.26.

12. Paul R. Abramson, *Political Attitudes in America* (San Francisco: W. H. Freeman, 1983), chap. 16.

13. Miller and Traugott, *Sourcebook,* 307, table 5.26.

14. Ibid.

15. Ibid.

16. Anthony Downs, *An Economic Theory of Democracy* (New York: Harper and Row, 1957), chaps. 3 and 14, and Norman Frohlich and Joe A. Oppenheimer, *Modern Political Economy* (Englewood Cliffs, N.J.: Prentice-Hall, 1978), chap. 5.

17. Ronald Inglehart, "Political Action: The Impact of Values, Cognitive Level, and Social Background," in *Political Action,* ed. Samuel H. Barnes and Max Kaase (Beverly Hills, Calif.: Sage, 1979), 370–377.

18. See, for example, Richard E. Dawson, Kenneth Prewitt, and Karen S. Dawson, *Political Socialization* (New York: Praeger, 1973), chap. 4. For evidence of the important but limited effects of the family as an agent of political socialization, see M. Kent Jennings and Richard G. Niemi, *The Political Character of Adolescence* (Princeton: Princeton University Press, 1974); and M. Kent Jennings and Richard G. Niemi, *Generations and Politics: A Panel Study of Young Adults and Their Parents* (Princeton: Princeton University Press, 1981), chap. 4.

19. M. Margaret Conway, Mikel L. Wyckoff, Eleanor Feldbaum, and David Ahern, "The News Media in Children's Political Socialization," *Public Opinion Quarterly* 45 (1981): 164–178; and M. Margaret Conway, David Ahern, and Mikel L. Wyckoff, "The Mass Media and Changes in Adolescents' Political Knowledge during an Election Cycle," *Political Behavior* 3 (1981): 69–80.

20. C. Anthony Broh, "Horse Race Journalism: Reporting the Polls in the 1976 Campaign," *Public Opinion Quarterly* 44 (1980): 514–529; Thomas E. Patterson, *The Mass Media Election* (New York: Praeger, 1980), chaps. 3 and 11; and Doris A. Graber, *Mass Media and American Politics* (Washington, D.C.: CQ Press, 1980), 178–180. The media also may be biased in their coverage of candidates based not only on their perceived electability but also on their social characteristics. See C. Anthony Broh, *A Horse of a Different Color: Television's Treatment of Jesse Jackson's 1984 Presidential Campaign* (Washington, D.C.: Joint Center for Political Studies, 1987).

21. Martin Levin, "Social Climate and Political Socialization," *Public Opinion Quarterly* 35 (1961): 596–606.

22. Jennings and Niemi, *Generations and Politics.*

23. Steven E. Finkel, "Reciprocal Effects of Participation and Political Efficacy: A Panel Analysis," *American Journal of Political Science* 29 (November 1985): 891–913.

24. M. Kent Jennings, "Residues of a Movement: The Aging of the American Protest Generation," *American Political Science Review* 81 (June 1987): 367–382.

25. Dawson, Prewitt, and Dawson, *Political Socialization*, 99–100.

26. Dean Jaros, Herbert Hirsch, and Frederic J. Fleron, Jr., "The Malevolent Leader: Political Socialization in an American Subculture," *American Political Science Review* 67 (1968): 564–575.

27. Dawson, Prewitt, and Dawson, *Political Socialization*, 99–105.

28. Ibid., 105–112.

29. Conway and Feigert, *Political Analysis*, 168.

30. Benjamin B. Woman (ed.), *Dictionary of Behavioral Science*, 2d ed. (San Diego: Academic Press, 1989), 249.

31. Abraham Maslow, "A Theory of Human Motivation," *Psychological Review* 50 (1943): 370–396; and *Motivation and Personality* (New York: Harper and Row, 1954). For applications of Maslow's theory to political behavior, see Jeanne N. Knutson, *The Human Basis of the Polity* (Chicago: Aldine-Atherton, 1972); and Stanley Renshon, *Psychological Needs and Political Behavior* (New York: Free Press, 1974).

32. Thomas Hobbes, *The Leviathan*, ed. Michael Oakeshott (Oxford: Basil Blackwell, 1960).

33. See, for example, Seymour Martin Lipset, *Political Man: The Social Bases of Politics* (Garden City, N.Y.: Doubleday, 1960), 175.

34. Lawrence Z. Freedman, "Psychopathology of Assassination," in *Assassinations and the Political Order*, ed. William Crotty (New York: Harper and Row, 1971), 143–160.

35. See, for example, M. Margaret Conway and Frank B. Feigert, "Motivation, Incentive Systems, and the Political Party Organization," *American Political Science Review* 62 (1968): 1169–1183.

36. See the classic argument in Harold D. Lasswell, *Politics: Who Gets What, When, and How* (New York: Meridian, 1958), 13.

37. See Carole Pateman, *Participation and Democratic Theory* (Cambridge: Cambridge University Press, 1970); and Terrence C. Cook and Patrick Morgan, "An Introduction to Participatory Democracy," in *Participatory Democracy*, ed. Terrence C. Cook and Patrick Morgan (San Francisco: Canfield, 1971), 1–40.

38. The same logic can be extended to participation in decision making in the workplace. In some countries, such as West Germany and Yugoslavia, this kind of participation is mandated by law. The product expected of it is greater worker satisfaction with the job and higher productivity.

39. David C. McClelland, *The Achieving Society* (New York: Free Press, 1961).

40. Rufus Browning, "The Interaction of Personality and Political System in Decisions to Run for Office: Some Data and a Simulation Technique," *Journal of Social Issues* 24 (1968): 93–109.

41. Ibid.; and James David Barber, *The Lawmakers* (New Haven: Yale University Press, 1965).

42. James David Barber, *Presidential Character* (New York: Prentice-Hall, 1972), 11.

43. For critiques of Barber's theory, see Alexander George, "Assessing Presidential Character," *World Politics* 26 (1974): 234–282; Jeanne Knutson, "Personality in the Study of Politics," in *Handbook of Political Psychology*, ed. Jeanne Knutson (San Francisco: Jossey-Bass, 1973), 28–56; and James H. Qualls, "Barber's Typological Analysis of Political Leaders," *American Political Science*

Review 71 (1971): 168–211. For Barber's reply to Qualls's criticisms, see "Comment: Qualls's Nonsensical Analysis of Nonexistent Works," *American Political Science Review* 71 (1977): 212–225.

44. Inter-University Consortium for Political and Social Research, codebooks for 1970, 1972, and 1974 American National Election Studies.
45. Samuel Evans and Kai Hildebrandt, "Technical Appendix," in Barnes and Kaase, *Political Action,* 545, table TA.2, and 548–549, table TA.3.
46. Ibid., 552, table TA.4.
47. Max Kaase and Alan Marsh, "Political Action Repertory: Change over Time and a New Typology," chap. 5 in Barnes and Kaase, *Political Action.*
48. Max Kaase and Alan Marsh, "Distribution of Political Action," in Barnes and Kaase, *Political Action,* table 6.3.
49. Clark McPhail, "Civil Disorder Participation: A Critical Examination of Recent Research," *American Sociological Review* 36 (1971): 1058–1073.
50. Martin Fishbein, "Attitudes and the Prediction of Behavior," in *Attitude Theory and Measurement,* ed. Martin Fishbein (New York: Wiley, 1967), 477–492; and Alan Marsh and Max Kaase, "Measuring Political Action," in Barnes and Kaase, *Political Action,* 61–65.
51. Barnes and Kaase, *Political Action,* 374, fig. 12.8.
52. For more extensive discussions of the concept of alienation, see Ada W. Finifter, ed., *Alienation and the Social System* (New York: Wiley, 1972); and David C. Schwartz, *Political Alienation and Political Behavior* (Chicago: Aldine, 1973).
53. Ada W. Finifter, "Dimensions of Political Alienation," *American Political Science Review* 64 (1970): 390–391. A sense of political powerlessness would imply an absence of a sense of control over the political sphere on the part of the individual. One psychological need suggested as affecting political participation is the need for a sense of mastery or control, which varies among individuals both in level and scope. A sense of personal control can be defined as a belief in the individual's ability to control his or her own life. For a discussion of how the need for personal control affects political behavior, see Renshon, *Psychological Needs.*
54. Kenneth Keniston, *The Uncommitted: Alienated Youth in American Society* (New York: Harcourt, Brace and World, 1965), 453–454. Keniston defines alienation as "the explicit rejection, 'freely' chosen by the individual, of what he perceives as the dominant values or norms of his society," 455.
55. For a discussion of several types of alienation, see ibid., 455–465. See also Finifter, "Dimensions," 389–410.
56. Keniston, *Uncommitted,* 466.
57. Schwartz, *Political Alienation,* esp. chap. 4.

Chapter 4

The Political Environment and
Political Participation

The political environment in which citizens live can stimulate or depress participation in elections and in other political activities. Among the components of the political context of elections are the electoral system, with its various requirements for voter eligibility, and the election administration rules used in a state or community, including voter registration procedures, the form of the ballot, and the provisions governing the conduct of the balloting on election day. The particular candidates and the issues that are at the center of political conflict during a particular political era can also have an important impact on electoral and campaign participation.[1] The historical division of contending forces in the community, state, and nation influences patterns of political participation as well.[2]

Another contextual factor has been the development of direct-mail techniques of fund raising and changes in federal campaign-finance laws, which have induced a larger proportion of citizens to give money for the support of political parties, candidates, and causes.[3] Republican party organizations have been particularly successful in using direct-mail solicitations to obtain funds. A portion of these funds is used to promote increased levels of political participation, including not only voting but also campaign activities. The great increase in political action committees since the mid-1970s has also provided a vehicle for increased contributions by donors to political parties, candidates, and causes.[4]

Still another environmental factor is the number and types of organizations seeking to promote and facilitate political participation. The role of organizations as stimuli to political action was noted by de Tocqueville even in the early days of the republic.[5] More recently, cross-national research has demonstrated the importance of organizations in guiding political participation; particularly among low-status persons, organizational membership and activity lead to higher rates of participation. The research also suggests that social and political institutions may play a more important role in stimulating political activity in other democracies than in the United States.[6] Even in the United States, however, organizations act to mobilize citizens. In 1984, for example, a number of organizations and coalitions of organizations conducted voter-registration and voter-turnout drives.[7] Even if not deliberately attempting to mobilize their members politically, organizations expose their members to politically relevant stimuli and provide opportunities for political activity.[8]

This chapter discusses the impact of several aspects of the political environment on political participation in the United States. These include the effects of changes in the underlying patterns of political conflict and political coalitions, the role of political movements, the impact of the mass media's presentation of politically relevant material, and the effects of organizational membership and activities. Also examined is the impact of factors specific to particular elections: the candidates and the issues, the competitiveness of the election, and the conduct of the campaign itself.

Electoral Party Systems

Political parties serve as vehicles for structuring conflict in society, conflict over both the goals to be achieved through public policy and the means to be used to achieve those goals. During any one era in a nation's history, one set of issues tends to be the focus of conflict, remaining at the center of attention until the underlying problems are resolved or alleviated and then being replaced by another set. Corresponding to each of these eras (five have been distinguished in American history) is an *electoral party system,* each of which differs from the others not only in the issues that divide the contending parties, but also in the group composition of the coalitions that form the support base for the parties and in the style of politics predominating at the time.[9]

In the past, an electoral party system has begun with either a *converting* or a *realigning* election. In a converting election, the party that previously had a majority of support among the electorate wins, but the issue basis and group conflict patterns are permanently altered. In a realigning election, not only are the issues and coalitions altered, but a different party wins the support of a majority of the electorate and is able to retain it for a number of years. The period of dominance for each majority party has been approximately three or four decades.[10] One realignment, for example, occurred during the late 1920s and early 1930s and signaled the end of seventy years of Republican dominance (through two electoral party systems).

Six conditions have been suggested as bearing upon realignment which occurs as a consequence of a converting or realigning election. These are (1) the breadth and depth of public concern with a major, critical problem; (2) the ability of the proposed remedies for the problem to stimulate opposition; (3) the motivation and ability of the parties' leaders; (4) the division between the parties of contending groups in society; (5) the strength of citizens' allegiances to the existing political parties; and (6) the ability of the party that won the election to govern effectively (in the perceptions of its supporters) after it takes control of the government.[11] Realignment would be expected to occur, creating a new electoral party system, if an issue arises that substantially affects a large number of people, if that issue divides the electorate differently from the existing issue basis of societal conflict, and if the proposed solutions to the problem provoke strong resistance from a substantial number of citizens. If leaders exist who are skilled at exploiting the grievance and stimulating its effects in restructuring political conflict, and if there exists a large pool of weak party identifiers and political independents available to be attracted to a different party, then the potential for realignment is very high. However, realignment will occur only if the political leaders swept into power on the basis of the new pattern of conflict are subsequently perceived by their supporters as governing successfully.

A converting or a realigning election is not the only way in which realignment can take place. Realignment can also occur in a gradual process, called a *secular realignment*. In such a case, one election does not become the focal point for a sudden and intensely felt change in the issue basis of political conflict. Instead, change occurs over a period of years as a result of the changing distribution of public opinion on one or more issues.

Secular realignment may occur as a consequence of social changes that produce alterations in either the salience or the distribution of opinion on a particular issue. It may also result from social changes that alter the social-group characteristics of the society. Examples of such changes since the realignment of the 1930s include migration of farm workers to urban areas and industrial jobs; population movement from one region of the country to another, as has occurred with the growth of the sunbelt areas of the United States; and the entry of a majority of adult women into the paid work force. Some scholars argue that a secular realignment occurred in the United States during the 1970s and 1980s.[12]

The shift in patterns of voting support that result from a realignment may involve several different processes of change. One of these is political mobilization of persons who formerly did not participate in elections. Thus, one major feature of a realignment may be increased levels of political participation. Heightened concern with an issue and more intense group conflict could logically be expected to result in higher levels of participation. Indeed, one theory is that realignment occurs precisely through the mobilization of nonvoters or of newly eligible voters who have not previously voted or participated in other ways.[13] If we distinguish between core voters, who regularly vote; marginal voters, who occasionally vote; and nonvoters, who almost never vote; then realignment occurs because of the entry into the electorate of large numbers of previously marginal voters and nonvoters. Over time, the support of these two types of voters flows disproportionately to one of the two parties, changing the political balance of power between them. A variation on this scenario is that a new party replaces one of the existing parties, as occurred during the 1850s with the rise to power of the Republican party.[14]

An alternative hypothesis is that realignment comes about by the conversion of a substantial number of core voters from regular support for one party to regular support for the other. While a reverse flow of support may also take place, it is not enough to maintain the formerly dominant party in power.[15]

A third explanation for realignment is that it occurs as a consequence of the replacement of older members of the electorate by younger members who have a different set of interests and experiences. For example, those thirty and younger in 1988 were much more likely to identify with the Republican party than those who were older. While conversion of older members of the electorate from Democrat to Republican occurred during the 1980s, and some movement of independents to the Republican party also occurred, in 1988 the thirty-and-under age group provided a significant proportion of voters who identified themselves as Republicans.[16]

During the first electoral party system, which lasted from the 1790s to 1828, voter eligibility requirements were relaxed substantially. While participation increased during this period, there appears to have been a lag between eligibility to vote and exercise of the franchise. However, during the second electoral party system (1828–1860), the political conflicts of the time did generate increased levels of voting turnout.[17] One of the most traumatic experiences endured by this nation—the Civil War—inaugurated the third electoral party system (1860–1896). The intensity of issue concerns and the high levels of emotional commitment to the contending parties resulted in levels of political mobilization that have not since been matched in our history. The low degree of economic interdependence, relative isolation of many rural and small-town communities, social pressures for political conformity, and effectiveness of familial political socialization produced high levels of partisan commitment and political participation in rural areas.[18] In many urban areas, political machines were very effective in mobilizing support. Indeed, some scholars have suggested that the apparently high voter turnout rates found in many cities in that electoral era might have been due in part to extensive ballot-box stuffing.[19]

With the beginning of the fourth electoral party system in 1896, political participation in the United States began to move downward. Although turnout in 1896 was 5 percent higher than in 1892, turnout in subsequent elections declined significantly.[20] The political alignment of the fourth electoral party system produced a number of one-party states, with the South being Democratic and many states in the North, Republican. One interpretation of this system is that both parties were captured by business and wealthy agrarian interests, while the interests of working-class citizens were not represented by either party, and as a consequence, political participation declined among the working class.[21] Also contributing to the low rates of political participation in the South was the systematic denial of political rights for black citizens.[22]

A detailed analysis of the election of 1896 and subsequent elections in the fourth party system does suggest that the political realignment that occurred was the result of the entry of various groups into the ranks of the voting public and the withdrawal of others, and was not caused by conversion of one party's supporters into supporters of the opposition party.[23] The decline in participation during this period has sometimes been attributed to the inflow of two groups into the eligible electorate: women newly enfranchised by the Nineteenth Amendment to the Constitution and large numbers of immigrants. The argument is that, since political participation is a habit acquired over time, participation was low because of the inadequate political socialization of these groups. However, turnout declined from the high levels of the nineteenth century even before the women's suffrage amendment came into force (1920) and in areas where new immigrants rarely settled.[24]

The electoral demobilization of the fourth party system was moderated by a realignment that began at the end of the 1920s and was consummated by the New Deal in the 1930s, marking the beginning of the fifth party system. It may have been generated in large part through the mobilization of nonvoters, either those who were newly eligible or those who had previously been eligible but had not voted. One study suggests that half of those who became eligible to vote during the 1920s had not voted before the election of 1932.[25] An alternative hypothesis is that the New Deal realignment occurred primarily as a result of the conversion of former Republican party supporters into Democratic party adherents.[26] In any case, voter turnout increased up until 1960, then began to decline again.[27]

Some scholars argue that the United States entered a sixth party system during the 1980s. They maintain that the realignment occurred not through a critical election, such as triggered the creation of the previous electoral party systems, but rather through secular realignment. This realignment, creating the sixth electoral party system, was a result of all three processes previously discussed—conversion of some Democrats to the Republican party, mobilization of some independents to become Republicans, and the replacement of older, Democratic cohorts by younger (thirty and under) citizens who were much more likely to identify with the Republican party.[28] If such a realignment in fact occurred, one would expect turnout rates to be higher. But turnout rates did not increase during the 1980s. (See Table 1-1.) Of course, younger citizens are much less likely to vote than those who are older; therefore, we should not expect an increase in turnout to occur as a result of realignment through generational replacement. Thus, the suggested realignment may in fact have occurred, even without a resulting increase in voter turnout.

The nature of the lines of conflict has stimulated or deterred political participation among some elements of the electorate throughout American history. Thus, the nature of the issues at the center of political conflict and the variations in responsiveness to those issues among different groups in the society have altered both the patterns of political support and the levels of political mobilization. In turn, political mobilization and demobilization have played an important role in structuring the nature of the electoral party systems.

Political Movements

A functioning party system in a democracy requires some degree of consensus on basic values; conflict occurs primarily over the distribution of values in the society and not over the values themselves. However, if a society has a party system that does not adequately reflect all points of view, those who do not perceive their interests to be represented may decide that they have no effective means of participating and simply not engage in any political activities. Alternatively, they may engage in political activities outside of the party system. One form of such activity is a political movement. For example, some farmers perceived during the late 1970s that their interests were not adequately represented by either political party or by already existing interest groups. A group of these disgruntled farmers meeting over coffee in a southern Colorado restaurant decided to form the American Agricultural Movement (AAM). The farmers declared an "agricultural strike," received national media coverage, and formed a national organization that soon claimed to have more than forty state chapters and eleven hundred local chapters. Their protests against the farm policies of the Carter administration were expressed in such nontraditional ways as a "tractorcade" to the national capital.[29] A second "tractorcade" in 1979 resulted in violent confrontations with the police and substantial property damage. As a consequence of the AAM's lobbying efforts, federal agricultural policies were modified.

A political movement arises from the concerns and needs of citizens who feel that the government is unresponsive to their problems. At first, individuals perceive the problem as personal, but then they realize that others have had similar experiences and face a similar problem. Symbols of a diagnosis of its causes and prescriptions for its solutions evolve and are adopted. To work toward putting these solutions into effect, organizations are formed. Their methods may include protest activities—either peaceful or violent—and more traditional forms of political activity.[30]

Political movements may mobilize individuals who have not previously been active. For example, the civil rights movement in the South during the 1950s and 1960s stimulated political activity among many black citizens who were denied the right to vote and other civil rights because of discriminatory laws and election administration procedures. This activity was primarily in the form of peaceful protests. However, in March 1965, during a march from Selma to Montgomery, Alabama, to demand voting rights for the state's black citizens, local and state police attacked the marchers with nightsticks, cattle prods, and police dogs. Coverage of that violent confrontation on national television provoked Congress into enacting the Voting Rights Act of 1965 which has been a very effective instrument in assuring suffrage. After the right to vote was obtained, the forms of activity associated with campaigns for elective office engaged the energies of supporters of the civil rights movement.

Political activity has been marked by many other political movements during the past three decades. The movement brought into being by opposition to the Vietnam War was accompanied by frequent peaceful protest demonstrations and a few acts of violence aimed at symbols of economic and political authority or at the institutions perceived as engaging in activities supportive of the war. More recently, movements focusing on such issues as equal political and economic rights for women, legalized abortions, a freeze on the production of nuclear weapons, the use of nuclear power for the production of electricity, America's adherence to traditional values, and American military involvement in Central America have been active nationally. These movements often draw citizens into forms of participation they have not used before, such as attendance at rallies or marching in protest demonstrations, as well as stimulate participation by some citizens who have not been active in any way.

If a movement is successful in getting its demands fulfilled, it may eventually die. Frequently, however, movements evolve into traditional interest groups, engaging in a wide range of lobbying and related activities and encouraging their members to become involved in conventional politics. A new party may even arise out of a political movement. The Republican party, originating in the antislavery movement, is an example of a successful transition from political movement to major political party. Several minor parties in American history also originated in political movements.[31]

Some supporters of a political movement may believe that violent forms of political action are instrumental to the attainment of a desired outcome. To others, acts of violence appear symbolic, expressing a point of view in a very forceful fashion. During the Vietnam War, a splinter group broke off from the antiwar movement and formed a group that came to be known as the Weathermen that vandalized property, bombed government buildings, and attacked such symbols of the war as draft board offices.[32]

An example of a movement's efforts to stimulate traditional forms of activity is provided by the anti-abortion movement. One of its activities has been the targeting of pro-abortion members of Congress for electoral defeat. The movement has raised funds for political action committees that have run advertising campaigns calling for the defeat of incumbents who had not supported anti-abortion legislation, and it has conducted voter-registration and voter-mobilization campaigns. In 1978, the Iowa Pro-Life Action Council targeted the state's Democratic senator, Dick Clark, for defeat. The group distributed three hundred thousand leaflets urging a vote against Clark, placing them on the windshields of cars in church parking lots on the Sunday before the November election. Clark lost by a margin of about 3 percent of the total vote. A postelection poll conducted by Clark's campaign pollster found that about 4 percent of Iowa's voters had been persuaded to change their vote by the leaflets,[33] although it does not necessarily follow that the activities of the Pro-Life Council were decisive in the outcome. In 1980, the council adopted another tactic. Volunteers contacted registered voters to identify those holding anti-abortion views who were willing to cast a vote solely on the basis of a candidate's stand on the abortion issue. These potential single-issue voters were then asked to serve as volunteers in the movement's campaign against Iowa's other senator, John Culver. They received anti-Culver campaign literature and were the target of a voter mobilization drive. Culver, too, lost his bid for reelection, again by a margin of about 3 percent. Efforts of this kind undoubtedly increased political participation among those who supported the anti-abortion group's position.[34]

Policy Agendas and Political Campaigns

Mobilization to political participation can be brought about by a number of processes. Party, candidate, and interest-group organizations seek to identify potential supporters, make sure that they are registered to vote, and get them to the polls on election day. The use of phone banks to contact potential voters is a key tactic in many campaigns, and face-to-face contacts at shopping centers or in door-to-door solicitations are also used. In 1984, the Republican National Committee, using demographic data from the census and other data on past voting patterns, identified precincts that contained large numbers of unregistered voters who would be likely to vote Republican. Volunteers canvassed each of these precincts, either by making phone calls or by going from house to house, and provided voter-registration information and registration forms to those who indicated they supported President Reagan's reelection and were interested in registering to vote. The Republicans' goal was to register two million additional Republican voters by November 1984.[35] The goal was exceeded.

Several studies indicate that these electoral mobilization activities can have a significant impact on both electoral participation and vote choice, even though they may increase turnout by only 5 to 10 percent.[36] The effectiveness of registration drives is increased the closer to the election date that they are held.[37] The effect appears to be greater in primary elections than in general elections. For example, the proportion of registered voters among black residents of Chicago increased substantially during the mayoralty campaign in 1983, stimulated by the fact that there was a black candidate, Harold Washington, and by the activities of the candidates, other organizations, and the mass media.[38] Participation also increased in other cities as a consequence of the candidacy of minority or ethnic group members.[39] However, those registered by a group-based registration drive may be less likely to vote than those whose registration is self-motivated.[40]

The closeness of a contest also appears to have an impact on voter turnout. Those who perceive an election for an important office as being close are more likely to vote than those who do not perceive it as being close.[41] Turnout in state legislative contests is higher in races that are decided by a smaller margin of votes.[42]

Another factor affecting turnout is the number and importance of the offices being filled. Turnout is highest in presidential elections, lowest in local elections not held simultaneously with any national or state elections. Turnout is higher in gubernatorial elections when a U.S. Senate election is being held simultaneously than it is otherwise.[43]

Campaign spending by candidates, party organizations, or interest groups can also have a substantial impact on turnout.[44] However, studies of state legislative contests suggest that the impact declines after a certain threshold point is reached.[45]

Another factor facilitating political mobilization is a citizenry with a strong commitment to a mobilization organization, such as a political party. One measure of this factor is the proportion of those registering who declare a party affiliation at the time of registration. This of course differs between states that encourage voter registration by party and that use closed (party-registrant only) primaries, and those that do not, but in state legislative elections, districts with a higher proportion of declared partisans have higher rates of turnout.[46]

Another condition tending toward greater participation is a lower level of consensus on the issue agenda and on the outcomes preferred on the issues. The less the consensus and the less assured one party's candidates are of victory, the greater is the likelihood that a citizen's efforts directed at a member of a legislature or a vote in an election will have an effect on the outcome. We would therefore expect turnout to be higher in closely contested elections, and other forms of political participation, such as lobbying officials in the executive branch, to be more extensive on issues where the probable outcome is in doubt.

Perceptions of the closeness of an election are related to level of interest in and attentiveness to politics; those who are more interested and more attentive are more likely to perceive an election as being close. Thus political interest and attentiveness appear to be mobilizing factors in turnout.[47]

One view envisions the eligible electorate as forming concentric circles, with those who vote in the most elections in the center of the circle, and those who vote in no elections in the outermost ring. However, an examination of voting participation in ten elections (five primaries and five general elections), using a sample of 115,800 voters drawn from the files of Kentucky's voter-registration system, indicates that this image of voter participants is inappropriate. Only 3 percent of the electorate participated in all elections, and mean turnout among the sample was four or five elections. The decision to participate depends on such considerations as the offices being contested; whether referendum issues are on the ballot, and if so, what the issues are; characteristics of the candidates who are running, such as their popularity and their group identifications; the proportion of offices being contested by incumbents; and the competitiveness of the contests.[48]

Effects of the Mass Media on Political Attitudes

The impact of the mass media on political participation is a subject of continuing dispute. One controversy concerns the depth of coverage of governmental activities. A majority of Americans rely on television for political news.[49] But most local television stations present only limited coverage of state and local government activities,[50] and much of national news coverage focuses on momentary controversies or on crisis events.[51] Television news tends to concentrate on events that can be presented dramatically; "talking heads" are considered to be relatively unappealing to the viewers. Thus, continuing coverage of less dramatic events is avoided, even if these may have greater importance in the long run.[52] For example, debates on budgetary allocations usually receive superficial coverage, although they can have a greater impact on citizens' lives than many of the fleeting but more dramatic political incidents that obtain greater coverage.

The style of media coverage, as well as the selection of stories, may foster negative perceptions and cynical attitudes about government and politics, and some scholars suggest that these perceptions and attitudes tend to reduce involvement with government to the extent that it is possible in a modern society.[53] Surveys conducted since the 1950s show that the growth of television coverage of politics has been accompanied by a decline in political trust. The proportion of citizens who can be said to "trust" the government declined from 76 percent in 1960 to 32 percent in 1982, increased to 44 percent in 1984, but fell to 40 percent in 1988.[54] In another series of surveys, 50 percent of those questioned in 1966 reported they had "a great deal" of confidence in "the people running" the Supreme Court, and 42 percent had a great deal of confidence in the people running the Congress; by 1981, the proportion reporting a great deal of confidence had dropped to 29 percent for the Supreme Court and 16 percent for Congress. The executive branch of government fared almost as badly: 41 percent had a great deal of confidence in 1966 and 24 percent in 1981.[55] More recently, however, confidence in political institutions has apparently begun to rise.

In a series of questions used by Gallup since 1973, the decline in confidence in the Congress, but not the Supreme Court, is evident. In 1973, Gallup reported that 44 percent of respondents expressed "a great deal" or "quite a lot" of confidence in the Supreme Court; by 1988, the percentage expressing that level of confidence had increased to 56 percent. In contrast, only 35 percent indicated that level of confidence in the Congress in 1988, compared to 42 percent in 1973. Confidence in Congress declined from 1973 to 1983 when it reached a low of 28 percent indicating "a great deal" or "quite a lot" of confidence in the Congress.[56]

Can these declines in trust and confidence that took place after 1966 be attributed to the mass media? Several researchers have concluded that they can be, and they place the principal blame on television. Analysis of data from a 1968 survey indicates that those who rely primarily on television as their main or only source of political news are more cynical and have less understanding of politics than those who use several sources, including print media. This difference remains, although at a reduced level, even when comparisons are made among persons with the same level of education.[57] A study of the effects of a controversial CBS television documentary, "The Selling of the Pentagon," led to the conclusions that reliance on television as a primary source of news increases "(a) social distrust, (b) political cynicism, (c) political inefficacy, (d) partisan disloyalty, and (e) third party viability."[58]

The print media also have an impact, with people's exposure to higher levels of political criticism in newspapers resulting in lower levels of political trust and efficacy. Newspaper stories that give relatively greater emphasis to political conflict and controversy stimulate greater political distrust and lower levels of political efficacy, although levels of trust appear to be affected more than efficacy.[59]

If both print media and television focus on conflict and controversy and present criticisms of political leaders, why do we assign to television more of the blame for the decline in the attitudes that are important in stimulating mass political participation? The reason apparently is that exposure to political stories on television is inadvertent; if one is watching a television news program, one sees whatever the television news editors have decided to present on that program. By contrast, print media can be selectively "edited" by readers themselves. If individuals wish to read only the sports section and the comics, or only stories about political issues and events, they can do so.[60]

Of course, the events unfolding since the development of television as a mass medium for the presentation of news in the 1950s also partly account for the decline in public confidence in political leaders and the political process. The assassinations of a president and of other prominent figures, the long and ultimately unpopular Vietnam War, the resignation of a president in disgrace, recurrent cycles of economic recession and recovery, and a continuing series of international economic and political crises—all have provided news that is not only controversial or unpleasant but often complex and confusing to the average citizen. That exposure to political news has a depressant effect on those attitudes, such as political efficacy and partisan loyalty, which are important in stimulating political participation is thus not surprising. Most content of the news media, however important or trivial, is presented as significant and usually in a context of controversy and crisis. Furthermore, good news and positive outcomes receive far less coverage than the bad and the negative. In short, both the content of the news and the style of news coverage have had an important impact on citizens' attitudes.

Effects of the Mass Media on Political Participation

The news media have a direct impact on one form of political participation—voter turnout. This comes about through the media's presentation of campaigns in news broadcasts, through candidate-sponsored advertisements, and through programs devoted to candidate debates or forums. The media also affect turnout through citizens' reactions to predictions of election outcomes before or on election day.

Editors make judgments about who are the more important candidates and how extensive the coverage of different candidates and contests should be. Reporters offer interpretations of candidates' actions and ideas that influence the electorate's perceptions and attitudes and ultimately their decisions about whether to vote and for whom. For example, potential presidential candidates must be considered "viable" by the media in order to get sufficient news coverage; if candidates are taken seriously by the media, they find it much easier to raise campaign funds and build an effective organization.[61]

Media requirements also shape the timing and staging of campaign events. An appropriate visual background for a presidential candidate's statement about farm policy may require rousing the presidential candidate's media entourage for an early morning fifty-mile journey to the site of a picturesque barn.[62] The fact that only fifty seconds of the statement will be aired is not necessarily discouraging to the candidate's campaign managers, but it illustrates why news coverage is often confusing to citizens. Those fifty seconds may be all the coverage that issue will receive on television during the entire campaign, despite the importance and complexity of the issue.

The media tend to give unequal coverage to the candidates. In presidential primaries, for example, the general pattern is for the candidate judged by the media to have won one round of nominating caucuses and primaries to receive more than a proportionate share of television time and print column-inches during the period up to the next round of caucuses and primaries. In 1976, Democratic candidate Jimmy Carter was anointed by the media as the "winner" of the Iowa caucus and the New Hampshire primary, even though he received only about 28 percent of the votes cast in each case, and thereafter he benefited from a disproportionate amount of news coverage and went on to win the Democratic nomination.[63]

The conclusion of most research, however, is that media coverage does not change attitudes during a campaign. Why, then, is the pattern of media coverage important? To answer that we must first consider the effects of campaigns. Campaigns have several effects. Probably the most important is to structure perceptions of candidates, political parties, and the public policy agenda. Another is to crystallize or sharpen and elaborate already existing cognitive and affective elements relating to candidates or parties in such a way as to increase consistency among already existing attitudes and beliefs. A third is to reinforce existing attitudes and beliefs.[64] But even if the campaign does not change attitudes and beliefs, media coverage provides the major communications linkage through which the campaign impresses most citizens. Media coverage structures citizens' perceptions of the candidates and the issues, and these perceptions are interpreted within the context of existing attitudes and beliefs. If some citizens think that the need for a strong national defense is the most important problem facing the nation, and if one candidate is presented by the media as being more likely to support additional expenditures for national defense, that perception, structured by both what the candidates are saying and the media's coverage of the candidates, will affect those citizens' vote choices as well as their probability of voting.

Another important way in which information is presented to citizens is through paid advertisements, especially in the form of thirty-second or one-minute television "spots." These advertisements are apparently a major source of influence on the least informed and least interested citizens. They have a feature not found in television news itself—frequent repetition of a single theme, with the message being simply and vividly presented so that it becomes very familiar to and is easily remembered by these potential voters.[65]

Some evidence suggests that paid media may be more influential in primary elections than in general elections. In the primaries potential voters have less information about the candidates running (except in the case of a popular incumbent) and fewer alternative sources of information. Media influence also appears to vary with the visibility of the office; it has a greater impact in contests for less visible offices.[66]

The activities of candidates presented through the mass media can have an impact on citizens' familiarity with the candidates. In 1978, more than half the citizens in districts where an incumbent representative was seeking reelection reported having heard, seen, or read something about the representative in the mass media, while only 20 percent had personally talked with the incumbent or the incumbent's staff. While a vigorous challenger to an incumbent can help stimulate electoral participation, the challenger is usually much less visible. Such was the case in 1978, when four-fifths of those interviewed in a national study recognized the incumbent's name but only two-fifths recognized the challenger's. One-fifth of those surveyed reported having seen or read about the challenger in the mass media, so it appears that about half the recognition received by a challenger is attributable to media coverage and campaign advertising.[67]

Participation can be significantly affected by the way in which the media are used and by direct contacts with the candidates. In 1978, the likelihood of voting in the congressional elections could be determined just as well from patterns of citizens' contacts with the candidates and from the frequency of their use of the mass media in learning about the campaign as from their demographic characteristics and political attitudes.[68]

Studies of the news coverage of political campaigns indicate that the press concentrates on who is winning and losing (the "horse race") and on the strategies pursued by various candidates, rather than on the candidates' issue stands and competence to govern.[69] If the election is predicted to be close, that prediction stimulates interest in it. The cost-benefit calculations of citizens are affected, as they perceive an increased probability that their votes will affect the outcome. That such calculations influence the decision to vote has been demonstrated by several studies.[70] Thus, predictions by the mass media about the closeness of a contest can have significant impact on election-day turnout.

Predictions of the election outcome are also made both during the campaign and on election day itself. The latter especially have become quite controversial. Formerly, outcome projections were based on surveys of samples of voters taken days or even weeks before the election. Now, however, they can be based on interviews with randomly selected voters as they leave the voting place (exit polls), and predictions of the outcome can be broadcast on television on election day before the polling places have closed in some areas.

Several studies have examined the effects of these election-day predictions. Three of them concerned the 1964 presidential election, when Lyndon Johnson won a landslide victory over Barry Goldwater. That outcome had been predicted long before election day, however, so the effects of the election-day predictions were probably minimal. One study reported no effects on turnout, a second reported a 1 percent change in choice of candidate, and a third reported a 3 percent change in choice.[71] While effects found in the latter two studies could have made a difference in a close presidential election, they had no impact on the outcome of the 1964 contest. A study of the 1968 election found that 4 percent of those surveyed in the east and 7 percent surveyed in the west changed their turnout intention after hearing the election outcome projections; 6 percent in the east and 7 percent in the west changed their choice of presidential candidate.[72] It should be noted that, aside from their effects on the presidential election, changes in the level of turnout can have an impact on the concurrent congressional contests. A study of the effects of election-day predictions in 1972 concluded that they reduced turnout by 2.7 percent in the Pacific coast states. That translates into 337,000 votes in California, for example, or an average of 7,800 votes per congressional district—enough to determine the outcome of a close congressional contest.[73]

Appraisal of the effects of election-day projections of the 1980 presidential contest also provides support for the view that they can have a small but decisive influence on voting participation. The projections that year, as well as President Carter's concession speech, both of them coming before the polls closed in many states, reduced turnout in both the east and the west below what was predicted on the basis of preelection interviews.[74]

Election-day projections probably have their greatest impact in those elections where a close race for president is expected, but instead an easy victory materializes for one of the candidates. The failure of some members of the electorate to vote because of the supposedly clear outcome of the presidential contest can significantly affect the outcome of other contests. Two Democratic representatives who were defeated in 1980 blamed their loss on the failure of many Democratic voters to come to the polls after hearing the networks' presidential election outcome predictions or Carter's concession speech. However, a study of the party affiliation of those who did not vote after hearing the projections or the Carter speech suggests that the reduction in turnout was greater among Republicans than among Democrats.[75]

Another study concludes that the early call of the 1980 election had only a slight effect on turnout but a larger effect on the direction of the vote, with Democratic candidates being adversely affected at both the presidential and congressional levels. Contests in fourteen congressional districts were won by margins of victory smaller than the estimated impact in those districts of the television networks' early call of the presidential election outcome.[76]

Representatives of the television news media and some scholars dispute the conclusion that election-day projections are a significant deterrent to voting participation. Admittedly, problems exist in assessing the effects of election projections on turn-out and vote choice for different offices. Much of the research based on individual-level data is conducted one to two months after the election has been held, presenting problems of recall of when and if citizens heard election projections on election day. Improved research designs would greatly facilitate study of the effects of election-day projections on voter turnout and vote choice. Researchers also should focus on the differential effects of hearing election-day projections for various groups within the electorate. For example, are Democrats and Republicans equally affected in various types of districts? Are individuals in different occupations, social classes, races, or age groups similarly affected by hearing election-day projections? Research suggests that the political context intervenes between people hearing election-day projections and making the decision to turn out. Various aspects of the political context—the number and level of offices being contested, traditional electoral outcomes, and the presence or absence of referenda on the ballot—may modify the effects of hearing election-day projections.[77]

In summary, election-day projections of presidential elections appear to act as a deterrent to turnout among a small but significant proportion of the electorate, with the effects being greater when a close election is predicted. The effects are seen not only in the vote totals in the presidential contest but also in the outcomes of elections for congressional and state offices being held at the same time.

Extensive media coverage of an election helps stimulate turn-out by increasing the public's interest in the campaigns, while low levels of campaign coverage may contribute to low turnout rates and also decrease other forms of participation. On the other hand, the level of coverage is in part a function of news editors' perceptions of the level of public interest. Competition for viewers among local television stations and between local stations and cable television is quite intensive, and if the news editors believe that the campaign is not interesting to the viewers, they will allot only limited coverage to it. This explanation was offered for the low level of television coverage of the 1974 gubernatorial contest in California.[78]

What is the contribution of media coverage to rational voting decisions? One scholar has concluded that "the prevalence of negative information makes it seem that all of the candidates are mediocre, or even poor, choices. This negative case appears to be a major factor in many voters' decisions to stay home on election day." She continues:

Although it would be unfair to blame low voter turnout in primary elections on inadequate election news, interviews with voters show that poor coverage plays a significant part. People find election stories interesting, but they do not feel that these stories prepare them adequately to make choices. Media images depict campaigns as tournaments where voters sit on the sidelines and watch the bouts, waiting to see who is eliminated and who remains. Winning and losing are all important, rather than what winning and losing means in terms of the political direction of the country in general or the observer's personal situation in particular. Taking its cues from the media, the audience accepts election news as just another story, rather than as an important tale about real life with very direct impact on its own welfare.[79]

Do the mass media also have an impact on other forms of political participation? One argument is that the media provide information about events, issues, and organizations, and that by informing and alerting the public in this way, the media stimulate people to join or support organizations that engage in political activity, to contact public officials, to become involved in court suits to block government actions, or to contribute to a political action committee. One example of such media influence might be the formation of a chapter of Mothers Against Drunk Driving first in one area of one state and then, after both local and national media coverage, of more local and state chapters throughout the country.

Those skeptical of this function of the media argue that the political activities that receive extensive coverage are often remote from the citizen, occurring either in Washington or overseas. Coverage is intermittent and often after the fact; for example, important legislation may be reported on only *after* a crucial vote has been taken in the House or Senate. And those parts of the policy process that occur within the executive branch, such as the drafting of regulations to carry out the policy and the implementation and enforcement of the policy, normally receive little publicity in the mass media. Usually the issues are complex, the key actors unknown to ordinary citizens, and the relevant processes not sufficiently understood to facilitate effective participation. The elites most affected by the issue, if not already involved (which is unlikely), may be mobilized by media coverage, and perhaps also a small subset of that part of the public most likely to attend to the media's political content, but the mass public will usually not be induced to participate by the media's political coverage. In order for that to happen, an issue must be present over a substantial period of time. If it is highly salient to ordinary citizens, the media's continuing coverage of the issue may then have an impact. Issues that receive such continuing coverage over a long period are rare, however. Furthermore, for political mobilization to occur, the media must convey some idea of how the public can become involved and whom they should contact, and that information is usually not provided. One explanation for the success of some interest groups may be their effectiveness at putting their name before the public, so that they become identified as the mechanism for engaging in effective action on their particular issues.[80]

Summary

Some aspects of the political environment work to encourage various types of participation while others act to inhibit them. In the early stages of an electoral party system's evolution, forms of conventional participation tend to increase; then, as the conflicts are alleviated and tensions in society decrease, participation can be expected to decline. As new conflicts arise that are not adequately handled by the political system, participation in both conventional and unconventional political activities can be expected to increase.

One type of political participation that increases when certain groups perceive their problems as not being dealt with by the government is joining a political movement. Recent American history has witnessed many political movements; some have evolved into organized interest groups that emphasize electoral and lobbying activities, while others have continued to function as political movements, using such forms of action as protest marches and demonstrations.

Political mobilization can be stimulated by the electoral context, including such factors as the perceived closeness of the contest for an office; the appeal of the candidates; the perceived importance of an issue; and the activities of party, candidate, and interest-group organizations. While the impact of these mobilization efforts may be small, it can have a significant effect in close elections, on legislative outcomes, and on the decisions of bureaucrats charged with implementing or enforcing a policy.

The mass media must also be recognized as a key element in the political environment. The development of television and changing patterns of print news accessibility have had a significant impact on citizens' perceptions of government, politicians, and the political process.

NOTES

1. Lester W. Milbrath and M. L. Goel, *Political Participation*, 2d ed. (Chicago: Rand McNally, 1977), 137–140; Angus Campbell, "The Passive Citizen," *Acta Sociologica* 6 (1962): 9–21; Wayne Parent and Wesley Shrum, "Critical Electoral Success and Black Voter Registration: An Elaboration of the Voter Consent Model," *Social Science Quarterly* 66 (1985): 695–703.
2. Paul Kleppner, *Who Voted?* (New York: Praeger, 1982); and Thomas Jahnige, "Critical Elections and Social Change," *Polity* 3 (1971): 465–500.
3. In 1952, 4 percent of the citizens reported contributing funds to political campaigns, whereas 16 percent were contributing by 1980. Alan R. Gitelson, M. Margaret Conway, and Frank B. Feigert, *American Political Parties: Stability and Change* (Boston: Houghton Mifflin, 1984), 201, table 9.1.
4. M. Margaret Conway, "Republican Party Nationalization, Campaign Activities, and Their Implications for the Political Party System," *Publius* 13 (1983): 1–17; Frank J. Sorauf, *Money in American Elections* (Glenview, Ill.: Scott, Foresman, 1988), chap. 3.
5. Alexis de Tocqueville, *Democracy in America* (New York: Vintage, 1957), 1: 259–260; 2: 114–116, 123–125.
6. Sidney Verba, Norman H. Nie, and Jae-on Kim, *Participation and Political Equality* (Cambridge: Cambridge University Press, 1978), chap. 5.
7. Among them were the Republican National Committee, Southwest Voter Registration Project, League of Latin American Citizens, National Association of Social Workers, and League of Women Voters. More than sixty organizations joined in a coalition to register more women voters. Research indicates that between 85 and 95 percent of those who are registered to vote do so; therefore, the major hurdle in increasing voting participation may be getting citizens to register. See Robert Erikson, "Why Do People Vote? Because They Are Registered," *American Politics Quarterly* 9 (1981): 259–276. However, in 1984, turnout among those registered appears to have declined by approximately 3 percent; see Committee for the Study of the American Electorate, *Non-Voter Study 84–85*, January 7, 1985, 2. Between 1984 and 1988, the proportion of the electorate registered to vote declined by 1.7 percent, while turnout by those

registered fell by 2.7 percent. U.S. Department of Commerce, Bureau of the Census, "Voting and Registration in the Election of November, 1986," Series P-20, No. 414 (Washington, D.C.: U.S. Government Printing Office), table A and table B; and U.S. Department of Commerce, Bureau of the Census, "Registration and Voting in the Election of November, 1988," Series P-20, No. 435 (Washington, D.C.: U.S. Government Printing Office, 1989), table A.

8. Sidney Verba and Norman H. Nie, *Participation in America* (New York: Harper and Row, 1972), 186–187; Norman N. Nie, Sidney Verba, Henry E. Brady, Kay Lehman Schlozman, and Jane Junn, "Participation in America: Continuity and Change" (paper delivered at the annual meeting of the Midwest Political Science Association, Chicago, April 14–16, 1989).

9. See Jahnige, "Critical Elections"; and Gitelson, Conway, and Feigert, *American Political Parties*, 26–27, table 2.2.

10. For discussions of electoral party systems in American history, see James Sundquist, *The Dynamics of the Party System*, rev. ed. (Washington, D.C.: Brookings Institution, 1983); Walter Dean Burnham, *Critical Elections and the Mainsprings of American Politics* (New York: W. W. Norton, 1970); and Jerome Clubb, William H. Flanigan, and Nancy Zingale, *Partisan Realignment: Voters, Parties, and Government in American History* (Beverly Hills, Calif.: Sage, 1980).

11. Sundquist, *Dynamics*, chap. 3; Clubb, Flanigan, and Zingale, *Partisan Realignment*, chap. 1; and Gitelson, Conway, and Feigert, *American Political Parties*, 35–36.

12. John Petrocik, "Issues and Agendas: Electoral Coalitions in the 1988 Election" (paper delivered at the annual meeting of the American Political Science Association, Atlanta, August 31–September 3, 1989); Helmut Norpoth and Michael Kagay, "Another Eight Years of Republican Rule and Still No Partisan Realignment?" (paper delivered at the annual meeting of the American Political Science Association, Atlanta, August 31–September 3, 1989). An alternative view holds that secular realignments can best be described as *issue evolutions*, as issues develop that alter the political environment. As a consequence of that alteration, new patterns of voter support develop. Proponents of this view argue that the concept of issue evolution allows for more gradations of change in the political environment than does the concept of political realignment. See Edward G. Carmines and James A. Stimson, *Issue Evolution* (Princeton: Princeton University Press, 1989).

13. Kristi Andersen, *The Creation of a Democratic Majority, 1928–1936* (Chicago: University of Chicago Press, 1979).

14. See Sundquist, *Dynamics*, chap. 5.

15. See ibid., chap. 10, with reference to the role of conversion in the realignment of the 1930s.

16. Norpoth and Kagay, "Another Eight Years of Republican Rule and Still No Partisan Realignment?"; John R. Petrocik, "Issues and Agendas: Electoral Coalitions in the 1988 Election" (paper delivered at the annual meeting of the American Political Science Association, Atlanta, August 31–September 3, 1989). For the exposition of a general theory of realignment through generational replacement, see Paul Allen Beck, "A Socialization Theory of Partisan Realignment," in *The Politics of Future Citizens*, ed. Richard G. Niemi and Associates (San Francisco: Jossey-Bass, 1974), 199–219.

17. Charles E. Johnson, Jr., *Nonvoting Americans*, Bureau of the Census Current Population Reports, Series P-23, no. 102 (Washington, D.C.: Government Printing Office, 1980), 2, table A.

18. Kleppner, *Who Voted?*, chap. 3; and Marc V. Levine, "Standing Political Decisions and Critical Realignments: The Pattern of Maryland Politics, 1872–1938," *Journal of Politics* 38 (1976): 292–325.

19. See Philip Converse, "Change in the American Electorate," in *The Human*

Meaning of Social Change, ed. Angus Campbell and Philip E. Converse (New York: Russell Sage, 1972), chap. 8; Walter Dean Burnham, "Theory and Voting Research: Some Reflections on Converse's 'Change in the American Electorate,'" *American Political Science Review* 68 (1974): 1002–1023; and Philip E. Converse, "Comment on Burnham's 'Theory and Voting Research,'" *American Political Science Review* 68 (1976): 1024–1027.

20. Johnson, *Nonvoting Americans*, 2, table A, and 3, fig. 1.

21. Burnham, *Critical Elections*, chap. 2.

22. See Richard B. Claude, *The Supreme Court and the Electoral Process* (Baltimore: Johns Hopkins University Press, 1970); and V. O. Key, Jr., *Southern Politics* (New York: Vintage, 1949), chaps. 25–30.

23. Kleppner, *Who Voted?*, chap. 4.

24. Walter Dean Burnham, "The Changing Shape of the American Political Universe," *American Political Science Review* 59 (1965): 7–28.

25. Andersen, *Democratic Majority*, 70–71.

26. Robert S. Erikson and Kent L. Tedin, "The 1928–1936 Partisan Realignment: The Case for the Conversion Hypothesis," *American Political Science Review* 75 (1981): 951–962.

27. Johnson, *Nonvoting Americans*, 5, table B, and 6, fig. 3.

28. John Petrocik argues that the realignment of the 1980s had not by 1988 produced a Republican majority. His research suggests that the realignment was a function of shifts in support by many groups, most prominent among these being white southerners, Catholics, blacks, and the households of northern union members. In contrast, Martin Wattenberg argues that the shift in partisan realignment is a "hollow" realignment, with citizens basing judgments and allegiance more on candidates than on perceived differences in the parties' issue stands and competence to govern. Norpoth and Kagay conclude that generational replacement contributed to a secular realignment; the Republican party gained an increasing share of partisan identifiers by 1988, but it still lagged behind the Democrats in the proportion of the electorate declaring a partisan affiliation. See Petrocik, "Issues and Agendas"; Norpoth and Kagay, "Another Eight Years of Republican Rule"; and Martin Wattenberg, "The Hollow Realignment Continues: Partisan Change in 1988" (paper delivered at the annual meeting of the American Political Science Association, Atlanta, August 31–September 3, 1989).

29. Allan J. Cigler and John Mark Hansen, "Group Formation Through Protest: The American Agricultural Movement," in *Interest Group Politics*, ed. Allan J. Cigler and Burdett A. Loomis (Washington, D.C.: CQ Press, 1983), 86–88.

30. Harold D. Lasswell and Abraham Kaplan, *Power and Society: A Framework for Political Inquiry* (New Haven: Yale University Press, 1950), 241–242.

31. See Sundquist, *Dynamics*, chap. 5; and David Mazmanian, *Third Parties in Presidential Politics* (Washington, D.C.: Brookings Institution, 1974).

32. For a discussion of the Weathermen, public reaction to their activities, and subsequent changes in their strategies, see Robert Brent Toplin, *Unchallenged Violence* (Westport, Conn.: Greenwood, 1975), 18–120.

33. Marjorie Random Hershey and Darrell M. West, "Single Issue Politics: Prolife Groups and the 1980 Senate Campaigns," in Cigler and Loomis, *Interest Group Politics*, 44–46; and Marjorie Random Hershey, *Running for Office* (Chatham, N.J.: Chatham House, 1984), chaps. 6 and 7.

34. Hershey and West, "Single Issue Politics"; Hershey, *Running for Office*, chaps. 6 and 7. Elsewhere, the anti-abortion movement has used more unconventional forms of political action, including the picketing of abortion clinics and even some acts of violence. Unconventional forms of participation will be discussed in chaps. 6 and 7.

35. See, for example, Thomas B. Edsall and Haynes Johnson, "High Tech, Impersonal Computer Net Is Snaring Prospective Republicans," *Washington Post*, April 22, 1984, A1.

36. Bruce E. Cain and Ken McCue, "The Efficacy of Registration Drives," *Journal of Politics* 47 (1985): 1221–1230.

37. Gerald Kramer, "The Effects of Precinct Level Canvassing on Voter Behavior," *Public Opinion Quarterly* 34 (1970), 560–572; William Crotty, "The Party Organization and Its Activities," in *Approaches to the Study of Party Organizations*, ed. William Crotty (Boston: Allyn and Bacon, 1968), 268–306; Raymond E. Wolfinger, "The Influence of Precinct Work on Voting Behavior," *Public Opinion Quarterly* 27 (1963): 387–398; Daniel Katz and Samuel Eldersveld, "The Impact of Local Party Activity upon the Electorate," *Public Opinion Quarterly* 25 (1961): 1–24; Phillips Cutright, "Measuring the Impact of Local Party Activity on the General Election Vote," *Public Opinion Quarterly* 27 (1963): 372–386; and Phillips Cutright and Peter Rossi, "Party Organization in Primary Elections," *American Journal of Sociology* 64 (1958): 262–269. For a study that found contacts did not increase turnout, see John C. Blydenburgh, "A Controlled Experiment to Measure the Effects of Personal Campaigning," *Midwest Journal of Political Science* 15 (1971): 365–381.

38. Nathaniel Sheppard, Jr., "Black-Oriented Radio Key in Chicago's Election," *New York Times*, March 15, 1983, D24.

39. Wayne Parent and Wesley Shrum, "Critical Electoral Success and Black Voter Registration: An Elaboration of the Voter Consent Model," *Social Science Quarterly* 66 (1985): 695–703.

40. Cain and McCue, "The Efficacy of Registration Drives," 1226.

41. Warren E. Miller and Santa A. Traugott, *American National Election Studies Data Sourcebook, 1952–1986* (Cambridge: Harvard University Press, 1989), 307, table 5.26.

42. Gregory A. Caldeira and Samuel C. Patterson, "Contextual Influences on Participation in U.S. State Legislative Elections," *Legislative Studies Quarterly* 7 (1982), 376, table 2.

43. Gregory A. Caldeira and Samuel C. Patterson, "Getting Out the Vote: Participation in Gubernatorial Elections," *American Political Science Review* 77 (1983): 684–685.

44. Ibid., 675–689.

45. Caldeira and Patterson, "Contextual Influences," 369–378.

46. Ibid., 376–377.

47. Kenneth D. Wald, "The Closeness-Turnout Hypothesis: A Reconsideration," *American Politics Quarterly* 13 (1985): 643–651.

48. Lee Sigelman and Malcolm Jewell, "From Core to Periphery: A Note on the Imagery of Concentric Circles," *Journal of Politics* 48 (1986): 440–449.

49. Gitelson, Conway, and Feigert, *American Political Parties*, 239, table 10.1.

50. Graber found that local television news broadcasts mentioned state and local government in not more than 7 percent of their stories: Doris A. Graber, *Mass Media and American Politics*, 3d ed. (Washington, D.C.: CQ Press, 1989), 88, table 3-3.

51. Ibid., 83–84.

52. Ibid., 84–86.

53. Ibid., 172; and Austin Ranney, *Channels of Power* (New York: Basic Books, 1984), chap. 3.

54. This represents the proportion responding "always" or "most of the time" to the question "How much of the time do you think you can trust the government in Washington to do what is right?" *American National Election Studies, 1960 to 1982.*

55. Seymour Martin Lipset and William Schneider, *The Confidence Gap* (New York: Free Press, 1983), 48–49, table 2-1.

56. The Gallup Report, December 1988, #279, 30.

57. Michael J. Robinson, "American Political Legitimacy in an Era of Electronic Journalism: Reflections on the Evening News," in *Television as a Social Force*, ed. Douglass Cater and Richard Adler (New York: Praeger, 1975), 97–139.

58. Michael J. Robinson, "Public Affairs Television and the Growth of Political Malaise," *American Political Science Review* 74 (1976): 409–432.
59. Arthur H. Miller, Edie Goldenberg, and Lutz Ebring, "Type-Set Politics: Impact of Newspapers on Public Confidence," *American Political Science Review* 73 (1979): 67–84.
60. Shanto Iyengar and Donald R. Kinder, *News That Matters* (Chicago: University of Chicago Press, 1987).
61. See, for example, C. Anthony Broh, "Presidential Preference Polls and Network News," in *Television Coverage of the 1980 Presidential Campaign*, ed. William Adams (Norwood, N.J.: Ablex, 1983), 29–48.
62. Timothy Crouse, *The Boys on the Bus* (New York: Random House, 1973), 140.
63. Thomas E. Patterson, *The Mass Media Election* (New York: Praeger, 1980), chap. 5. See also John Aldrich, *Before the Convention* (Chicago: University of Chicago Press, 1980), 176–192.
64. For discussions of campaign effects, see Dan Nimmo, *The Political Persuaders* (Englewood Cliffs, N.J.: Prentice-Hall, 1970), 164–172; and George Comstock, Steven Chaffee, Nathan Katzman, Maxwell McCombs, and Donald Roberts, *Television and Human Behavior* (New York: Columbia University Press, 1978), 339–341. See also Graber, *Mass Media and American Politics*, chap. 6; Ranney, *Channels*, 80–86; and Patterson, *Mass Media Election*.
65. Thomas E. Patterson and Robert McClure, *The Unseeing Eye* (New York: Putnam, 1976), 116–120.
66. Michael J. Robinson, "The Media in 1980: Was the Message the Message," in *The American Elections of 1980*, ed. Austin Ranney (Washington, D.C.: American Enterprise Institute, 1981), 177–211.
67. M. Margaret Conway, "Mass Media Use, Candidate Contacts, and Political Participation in Congressional Elections" (paper delivered at the annual meeting of the Southern Political Science Association, November 6–8, 1980).
68. Ibid.
69. C. Anthony Broh, "Horse Race Journalism: Reporting the Polls in the 1976 Campaign," *Public Opinion Quarterly* 44 (1980): 514–529; and Patterson, *Mass Media Election*, chap. 3.
70. Norman Frohlich and Joe A. Oppenheimer, *Modern Political Economy* (Englewood Cliffs, N.J.: Prentice-Hall, 1978), chap. 5; and Gregory Brunk, "The Impact of Rational Participation Models on Voting Participation," *Public Choice* 35 (1980): 549–564.
71. Kurt Lang and Gladys Engel Lang, *Voting and Non-Voting* (Waltham, Mass.: Blaisdell, 1968); Harold Mendelsohn and Irving Crespi, *Polls, Television and the New Politics* (Scranton, Pa.: Chandler, 1970), chap. 4; and Douglas A. Fuchs, "Election Day Radio-Television and Western Voting," *Public Opinion Quarterly* 30 (1966): 226–236.
72. Sam Tuchman and Thomas E. Coffin, "The Influence of Election-Night Television Broadcasts in a Close Election," *Public Opinion Quarterly* 35 (1971): 315–326.
73. Raymond Wolfinger and Peter Linquiti, "Tuning In and Turning Out," *Public Opinion Quarterly* 4 (1981): 57–58.
74. John E. Jackson, "Election-Night Reporting and Voter Turnout," *American Journal of Political Science* 27 (1983): 615–635.
75. Ibid., 620–621.
76. Michael X. Delli Carpini, "Scooping the Voters? The Consequences of the Networks' Early Call of the 1980 Presidential Race," *Journal of Politics* 46 (1984): 866–885.
77. J. Ronald Milavsky, Al Swift, Burns W. Roper, Richard Salant, and Floyd Abrams, "Early Calls on Election Results and Exit Polls: Pros, Cons, and Constitutional Considerations," *Public Opinion Quarterly* 49 (1985): 1–18; Seymour Sudman, "Do Exit Polls Influence Voting Behavior?" *Public Opinion*

Quarterly 50 (1986): 331–339; Ronald J. Busch and Joel A. Lieske, "Does Time of Voting Affect Exit Poll Results?" *Public Opinion Quarterly* 49 (1985): 94–104.

78. Mary Ellen Leary, "California 1974: The Browning of Campaign Coverage," *Columbia Journalism Review* 15 (1976): 18–21.
79. Graber, *Mass Media and American Politics*, 181–183.
80. James B. Lemert, Barry N. Mitzman, Michael A. Seither, Roxana H. Cook, and Regina Hackett, "Journalists and Mobilizing Information," *Journalism Quarterly* 54 (1977): 721–726.

Chapter 5

The Legal Structure and Political Participation

This chapter will examine, first, the ways in which the rules determining eligibility to vote and the laws and procedures governing the conduct of elections affect electoral participation, and then the effects of governmental structure, practices, and regulatory procedures on other forms of political participation.

The Struggle for the Right to Vote

Ordinary citizens gained the right to participate in elections only after a long struggle. Even today, only one-fourth of the world's nations have competitive, free elections in which the people really decide who shall govern.[1] The motto of the American Revolution, "No taxation without representation," expressed the deep commitment of the nation's founders to what they considered to be a natural right. The United States was the first nation to have mass suffrage and competitive free elections, although in recent years the right to vote has been exercised by only about half its citizens, even in elections for national offices (see Table 1-1). In state and local elections, substantially less than half the eligible electorate votes.

The founders of the United States set out to create not a "democracy" but a "republic," in which sovereign power would reside in a restricted electorate and be exercised by the electorate's representatives. Many of the nation's early leaders believed that ordinary citizens lacked the knowledge and wisdom necessary to participate in governing. Others, however, thought otherwise, and the question of who should have the right to vote generated such disagreement in the Constitutional Convention in 1787 that the decision was left to the states.[2] The Constitution simply declared (Article 1, section 2) that any person who was eligible to vote in elections to the most numerous branch of a state's legislature was also eligible to vote in elections to the federal House of Representatives. However, Article 1, section 4, gave Congress the power to enact laws concerning the "times" and "manner" of holding elections for its members.

Before the Revolution, only those who owned property could vote in the colonial elections, and the newly formed states continued to impose this restriction on access to the ballot. The colonies had been formed as business corporations, and an individual was not considered to be a member unless he owned property in the corporation. As the colonies evolved into political entities, some of them imposed additional restrictions on suffrage, including criteria relative to race, age, sex, color, and religion. For example, both Jews and free nonwhites were forbidden to vote in several colonies, and others excluded Catholics from the vote. In some of the colonies, mainly in New England, a potential voter had to prove that he met standards of "good character." After the colonies joined together to form the United States, some of these restrictions on eligibility to vote were continued.[3]

Property restrictions were usually stated in terms either of the value of the property or of the number of acres owned.[4] In some states, a minimum level of wealth remained a condition for eligibility for more than fifty years after the ratification of the Constitution, although the requirement was later more likely to be stated in terms of the amount of taxes paid than of the amount of property owned.[5]

Even after property ownership and taxpaying conditions were eased or eliminated, turnout rates remained low. In the 1828 presidential election, only about one-fifth of the nation's adult population voted, but, of course, women and nonwhite males did not have the right to vote at that time. In the presidential election of 1844, the first one in which no state had a property or taxpaying requirement for voting, a little less than 31 percent of the adult population voted. Until 1920, the highest level of turnout was in the election of 1876, when 37.1 percent of the adult population cast votes; that election focused on economic issues and the end of Reconstruction in the South.[6] Voter turnout as a proportion of the eligible electorate was higher during the latter part of the nineteenth century than at any other time in American history. It began to decline after the political realignment of 1896 and has never returned to that high level.

Women's Suffrage

Women did not have the right to vote in colonial America. In 1787, Abigail Adams, the wife of John Adams, wrote to him asking that he "remember the ladies" and advocating women's right to vote.[7] Her plea was ignored. Actually, the struggle for women's suffrage had begun even earlier. Margaret Brent, a wealthy resident of Maryland, had petitioned the Maryland Council in 1647 for the right to vote. She was the agent and legal representative of Lord Baltimore, the proprietor of the Maryland colony, and the executrix of the estate of Leonard Calvert, the deceased brother of Lord Baltimore. Appearing before the colonial council, she demanded that it grant her not one but two votes, one as the executrix of Calvert's estate and the other as Lord Baltimore's representative. She argued that if she was not granted two votes, all proceedings of the council would be invalid. Not persuaded by her arguments, the council denied her request.[8]

Women were not excluded by law from voting at this time, because it did not occur to most men that women would want to vote or attempt to vote. However, in a few local communities some women of prominent families did participate in elections, and it became such a common occurrence that state laws were enacted late in the eighteenth century to prohibit it. In New Jersey, no law excluding women from the suffrage was enacted until 1807, when it appeared that women's votes might influence the outcomes of elections in a direction opposed by those holding political power in the state.[9]

In the nineteenth century, women began an organized campaign to obtain the right to vote. Through their participation in the abolitionist movement, women learned to organize, speak in public on political issues, and conduct campaigns to gain support for a policy. Furthermore, many women employed in the factories and textile mills actively protested the wretched conditions in which they worked. Although their protests were unsuccessful, they, too, learned how to organize, petition, and lobby.[10]

The antislavery movement also helped generate the leadership of the women's movement. In 1840, a world antislavery convention was held in London, attended by both male and female delegates from the United States. The convention ruled, over the protests of the U.S. delegates, that women could not be delegates to the convention and would have to take seats in the spectators' galleries.[11] Among the American women attending the convention were Lucretia Mott and Elizabeth Cady Stanton, and their experience led them to discuss the condition of women in the United States and the world. Some of the ideas underlying the women's movement took form then, and Mott and Stanton became its first leaders. Later, Stanton moved with her family to the small town of Seneca Falls, New York. Burdened by housework and child care, without servants to help her and with a husband often away traveling on business, she came to resent her situation and recognized that many other women shared her circumstances. She expressed her resentment in a small advertisement that she placed in the *Seneca County Courier,* calling for a Women's Rights Convention to meet in the Wesleyan Chapel on July 19 and 20, 1848. The convention issued a "declaration of principles" and drafted a set of resolutions to implement it. The declaration and accompanying resolutions are recognized as the beginning of the women's rights movement in the United States; they state the issues that were the focus of the movement and that set the public-policy agenda for women in the nation.[12]

As the struggle for women's rights continued, gains were made after the Civil War in areas such as free public elementary and secondary education, and a few colleges admitted a limited number of women. Gradually, the strategy evolved of emphasizing the acquisition of political rights, with the right to vote considered to be the key to success in obtaining other rights.[13] Widows with school-age children had been granted the right to vote in Kentucky's school elections in 1838, but the next state to enfranchise women in school elections, Kansas, did not do so until 1861. Granting women the right to vote in school elections was regarded as a natural extension of their role as mothers, and twenty-six states had extended suffrage to that extent by 1920. However, support for full suffrage rights for women does not appear to have been closely related to granting the right to vote in school elections.[14]

Women first obtained full suffrage in all elections in the territory of Wyoming in 1871, and this provision was retained when Wyoming became a state in 1890. As the leaders of the women's movement had predicted, other rights came with the right to vote. The women of Wyoming also gained the right to serve on juries, to exercise control over their own property, and not to be discriminated against in employment as teachers. By 1918, full women's suffrage had been granted in fourteen other states (all but one of them, New York, being western states), and by the end of 1919, eleven more states had followed suit.[15] The women's suffrage amendment to the national Constitution was proposed by Congress in 1919 and was certified as having been ratified by the requisite thirty-six states in August 1920.

What were the major factors that led to the adoption of the women's suffrage amendment? One was that twenty-six states already permitted women to vote by that time. The second was the strategy pursued by women's rights leaders, such as Carrie Chapman Catt, of presenting the issue as one of equity, not of role change. Third, women had played active roles in World War I, working in the war relief effort and taking employment in nontraditional occupations as replacements for men who had gone into military service. Fourth, Mrs. Catt had obtained the active support of President Woodrow Wilson by supporting his policies both during and after the war. Women's rights leaders also sought his advice on the strategy and tactics of their campaign. Finally, women's suffrage became a component of the Progressive-era reform movement, which had middle-class support.[16]

The opposition to women's suffrage at the turn of the century had come from several sources. These included southern political leaders, who were inheritors both of a patriarchal culture and of memories of northern women's strong support for the antislavery movement, and conservative church leaders, drawn primarily from the Catholic church and fundamentalist Protestant sects. Some business interests also opposed women's suffrage, fearing that women voters would support child-labor laws and the legal recognition of unions. Political bosses, believing that women would support reforms in the political process that would weaken the power of their political machines, were often opposed. Finally, the liquor and brewery interests thought that women would support a constitutional amendment to forbid the manufacture and sale of alcoholic beverages. But by 1919, child-labor regulations, political reform, and prohibition had already been enacted, without benefit of women's votes, and so some of the opposition to women's suffrage weakened.[17]

After women obtained the right to vote, many of them nevertheless did not immediately exercise it. Voting is an acquired habit, which must be learned over time and through experience. Those intimidated by past cultural norms were slow to learn the value of the vote. Although the Nineteenth Amendment came into force in August 1920, several states did not reopen their voter registration rolls to allow women to register to vote in that year's presidential election. And finally, many women faced difficulties in getting to voter registration offices because of their household and child-care responsibilities; the necessity of traveling to register at a county courthouse, township office, or city hall which was usually open only during working hours on weekdays; and the limited means of transportation. Gradually, however, women began to participate in elections in larger proportions, and the difference between men and women in turnout rates seems now to be disappearing (see Chapter 2).

Minority Suffrage

Members of minority groups also endured the denial of their political rights. Although the Fifteenth Amendment to the Constitution formally ended racial barriers to the vote in 1870, effective enfranchisement both for most black citizens living in the South and for minority citizens living in some other areas did not come until after passage of the Voting Rights Act in 1965. The Fifteenth Amendment specified that "the right of citizens of the United States to vote shall not be denied or abridged by the United States or by any state on account of race, color, or previous condition of servitude." The second section of the amendment gave Congress the power to enact legislation to enforce that policy. However, several laws enacted by Congress in the 1870s, which sought to put a stop to acts of violence and intimidation aimed at preventing black citizens from voting, were narrowly interpreted by the U.S. Supreme Court and proved to be ineffective.[18]

A number of methods were used in the southern states to prevent minority citizens from voting. One was the poll tax, which had to be paid before a citizen could register to vote. Though often a seemingly nominal sum, the tax was nevertheless a burden to those of very low income, and in effect it made voting a luxury not only for poor blacks but for poor whites as well. The tax often had to be paid many months before an election, and therefore it also disenfranchised newcomers to the district or those absentminded citizens who forgot to pay it.[19]

Another device was the literacy test, which required that citizens demonstrate their ability to read and interpret a specific document, such as the state or the federal constitution. Considering the problems that judges often have in agreeing how a constitutional provision should be interpreted, this requirement, even if administered fairly, could be difficult to meet—and voting registrars in many southern states failed to administer it fairly. In addition, some states attempted to exempt white citizens from the literacy requirement altogether by specifying that men who had been eligible to vote before a specified date, as well as their sons and grandsons, could continue to vote in any case. The Supreme Court eventually struck down this so-called "grandfather" clause.[20]

A third device used to prevent black citizens in the South from voting was the "white primary." After the end of Reconstruction, the Democratic party became the dominant party in most parts of the South. Thus, the important decision point in the election process was the Democratic party's nominating convention or primary election. In 1923, Texas enacted a law stating that only white citizens could vote in the Democratic party's primary. This law was overturned by the Supreme Court in 1927,[21] but the Texas legislature then passed a law giving the Democratic party the right to specify who was eligible for party membership and participation in party activities. The Supreme Court struck down that law in 1932.[22] Other southern states adopted similar measures. However, in 1941 the Supreme Court ruled that primary elections are subject to federal control if they are an integral part of the election process and if they effectively determine the choices available to voters in the general election, and in 1944 the white primary was held to be a violation of the Fifteenth Amendment.[23]

Violence was also used to deny voting rights to black southerners. During Reconstruction, a secret society—the Ku Klux Klan—was organized in the South, and among its principal activities were threats or acts of violence and economic coercion aimed at intimidating black citizens into refraining from exercising their political and other civil rights.[24] These practices continued well into the twentieth century—indeed, in some areas of the South, even after the passage of the 1965 Voting Rights Act.[25] This act made it a federal crime to threaten, intimidate, or coerce or to attempt to threaten, intimidate, or coerce people to prevent them from exercising their right to vote.[26] Unfortunately, however, a general climate of intimidation, and especially use of the threat of economic retaliation, is both difficult to overcome and difficult to prove in court.

Southern political leaders whose own political interests were served by the exclusion of blacks from effective political participation tried to prevent federal protection of the rights of black citizens. One way was by use of the tradition of unlimited debate in the Senate to kill proposed civil-rights legislation by filibustering against it. After the Democrats gained a majority in Congress in the election of 1932, southern Democrats used their positions of leadership in congressional committees to block such legislation. A third mechanism was the Democratic party's requirement, which was in effect until 1936, that a presidential candidate must receive two-thirds of the votes in the convention in order to win the nomination, a provision that gave the South an effective veto in the Democratic party's presidential nominating process.[27]

The systematic denial of minorities' basic political rights came under increasing attack during the 1950s and 1960s. Four national laws, a constitutional amendment, extensive litigation, and vigorous federal enforcement were all parts of a broad effort to assure the right to vote to all citizens. The first civil-rights law enacted in the modern era was the Civil Rights Act of 1957, which authorized the attorney general to seek court injunctions on behalf of specific individuals whose right to vote had been interfered with on the basis of race. If, for example, a black citizen tried to register to vote in a southern county and was subsequently fired from his job, the attorney general could apply for an injunction to have the citizen's job restored. But such suits had to be filed in the federal district court in whose jurisdiction the intimidation took place, and some southern federal district judges were slow to act on these cases. Furthermore, the victims of the discriminatory acts were hesitant to become involved in legal proceedings. The 1957 act also established the Civil Rights Commission and the Civil Rights Division of the Department of Justice and extended the jurisdiction of the federal district courts in civil cases. Nevertheless, it did not prove to be effective in securing voting rights for all Americans.

Consequently, another civil-rights statute was enacted in 1960, giving the attorney general the right to file suits against states as well as against specific individuals, such as local voting registrars.[28] This expansion of federal authority was deemed necessary because in some states voting registrars had resigned and not been replaced, leaving no one who could be sued to end discriminatory practices. The 1960 act also authorized the federal courts to appoint voting referees, who could register voters in a particular county if the court found a pattern or practice of discrimination there.[29] The problem, however, was that these remedies had to be applied on a case-by-case basis. The proceedings were often very slow, and some southern federal district court judges were reluctant to find a pattern of discrimination. Thus, the 1960 law still did not bring an end to racial discrimination in access to the ballot box.

In the Civil Rights Act of 1964, Congress attempted to ensure that literacy tests, where used, would be administered fairly. The law required each state to establish a uniform set of standards, procedures, and practices for the administration of elections. Completion of a sixth-grade education was to be considered sufficient proof of literacy for eligibility to vote in a federal election. When literacy tests were used, they had to be individually administered in writing, with a copy of the test and its results made available within twenty-five days to the individual who had taken it and a copy retained by the voting registrar as part of the official records.

These provisions, however, still did not end the abuse of literacy tests and the use of other discriminatory tactics. Therefore, the Voting Rights Act of 1965 suspended the use of literacy tests in all states or counties where less than 50 percent of the voting-age population of the state or county was registered to vote as of November 1, 1964. The act authorized the appointment of federal examiners to evaluate the qualifications of persons seeking to register to vote in those areas. Eligible persons would be registered, and lists of those registered were to be provided to state election officials. The act was initially to be in effect for a period of five years, but in 1970 it was extended for another five years, in 1975 for eight years, and in 1982 for twenty-five years.[30] The act and its extensions have been highly effective in the fight against the discriminatory administration of election laws. Racial differences in the proportion of the voting-age population that is registered to vote have greatly declined, though they have not been entirely eliminated (see Table 5-1).

Registration and Election Procedures

Even fairly administered election laws and procedures may constitute obstacles to voting. The extent to which they do is a function both of the nature of the laws and procedures and of certain characteristics of members of the electorate.

TABLE 5-1
*Voter Registration by Race in 11 Southern
States, 1960, 1970, 1980, and 1988*

| | Percent of voting-age population registered | |
	White	Black
1960	61.1	29.1
1970	56.0	43.5
1980	65.8	56.5
1988	66.6	63.3

SOURCES: U.S. Bureau of the Census, *Statistical Abstract of the United States, 1982–1983* (Washington, D.C.: Government Printing Office, 1984), 488, table 799. For 1988 data: U.S. Bureau of the Census, "Registration and Voting in the Election of November, 1988" (Advance Report), Current Population Reports, Series P-20, No. 435 (February 1989), 3, table C.

Comparisons of voter turnout rates among states within the United States and between the United States and other countries reveal that obstacles to voting created by election administration procedures do have a depressing effect on turnout. Furthermore, in states or countries where the costs to vote are higher in time, information, and effort, individuals with fewer resources are less likely to vote, unless lack of resources is offset by the political-mobilization effects of group memberships and group activity.[31] In effect, then, election procedures common in the United States work to create a class bias in voter turnout. Middle- and upper-class citizens are more likely to vote than are working-class citizens.[32] Educational attainment is an important determinant of who votes, and one reason is that those with more education usually are better able to cope with the bureaucratic hurdles created by the registration and election-administration procedures.[33]

Voter turnout in the United States lags substantially behind the rates found in other developed democracies. One study of voter turnout reports that during 1972–1980 an average of 80 percent of the eligible electorate residing in twenty developed democracies voted; during the same period the average turnout in the United States was 54 percent.[34] Compared to other developed democracies, however, the United States has a political culture that is more supportive of political participation: Americans are more likely to consider themselves close to a political party, to feel efficacious about politics, and to express at least some interest in politics, although they are less likely to express trust in government. Citizens of the United States are also more likely to discuss politics with others, to try to convince others how to vote during an election, and to work for a candidate or party. Demographic characteristics associated with higher levels of voting turnout are also more prevalent among Americans; these characteristics include more persons with higher levels of education and more occupying white-collar jobs.[35] Why, then, are Americans much less likely to vote than the citizens of other countries?

Political scientists generally agree that voter-registration and election-administration laws, as well as characteristics of the political party and governmental system, contribute to reduced voter turnout in the United States. They disagree, however, concerning how much of the low voter-turnout levels can be attributed to institutional arrangements as opposed to political culture. One study by G. Bingham Powell concludes that the absence of nationally competitive election districts and the weakness of links between various societal groups and the party system, together with the presence in the electorate of a large number of younger voters, contributed significantly to lower turnout in the United States from 1971 to 1980. Also significant in the previous decade (1961–1970) were the absence of automatic registration procedures or government-conducted registration. Aspects of American political culture, such as higher levels of interest in politics, a widespread sense of political efficacy, and a relatively well-educated electorate, increased participation by about 5 percent. However, Powell estimates that the necessity for American citizens to take the initiative to register themselves decreased voting turnout by 16 percent during the 1970s. Other factors that helped decrease turnout were the low level of linkage between American political parties and groups in the society (an estimated 10 percent reduction) and the low competitiveness of elites (reducing turnout by 3 percent). To summarize, Powell concludes that cultural factors, such as higher levels of education, political interest, and efficacy, increased turnout in the United States while others—especially low party-group linkage and the necessity for self-registration—significantly reduced turnout below levels found in other developed democracies.[36]

Other scholars have argued that political and institutional arrangements, not such aspects of political culture as levels of interest and efficacy, foster lower voter turnout. Robert W. Jackman, for example, examined the same developed democracies as Powell, with the single exception of Spain (which he excluded) and used data from the same decades. Jackman reports that five institutional factors contribute to *increasing* turnout: (1) mandatory voting, (2) a unicameral legislature, (3) a two-party system as opposed to a multi-party system, (4) nationally competitive districts, and (5) a lower level of disproportionalities in translating votes cast into seats won in the lower house of the national legislature. While multiparty systems offer the voters more choices, Jackman argues that institutional arrangements that allow the electorate a more direct role in the formation of the government, as a two-party system does, are more likely to stimulate turnout.[37]

Voter-registration systems were established to ensure that only those who were legally entitled to vote did so and that each voter cast only one ballot in each election. Most countries limit eligibility to vote to their own citizens and to those who have reached a minimum age. In the United States, citizens must also be legal residents of the state in which they vote in order to be eligible.[38]

During the 1960s and 1970s, many registration procedures were changed to make it easier for citizens to vote. Some of these changes were made by state legislatures seeking to encourage voting participation; others were imposed by the courts because some state election-administration laws violated the federal Constitution. For example, the Supreme Court has ruled that, except in rare circumstances, registration books should close no earlier than thirty days before an election.[39] The length of residency required has also been shortened in many states.[40]

The registration process amounts to a major barrier to voting. Those who do not register cannot vote, while those who do register are highly likely to vote. Surveys conducted by the Center for Political Studies at the University of Michigan showed that 94 percent of those who were registered voted in the 1964 presidential election; in 1976, the figure was 88 percent.[41] In 1982, only three-fourths of those registered voted—but even more important, 36 percent of those who were otherwise eligible to vote were not registered.[42] In 1988, 66.6 percent of those eligible were registered, and 86 percent of those registered voted. Thus, the decline in voting turnout in the United States has worsened both because a lower percentage of those eligible are registered and because fewer of those registered are voting than in the past.[43] The great majority of nonvoters come from the ranks of those who are not registered.

Early voter-registration laws authorized local officials to prepare registration lists on the basis of existing lists and their own knowledge of community residents. A citizen did not have to apply personally in order to be registered.[44] The problem with this system was that it permitted errors of both omission and commission. Some eligible voters were missed, while local officials could list as eligible persons who had died, who lived in some other district, or who simply did not exist. These defects led to the establishment of registration systems in which an individual had to make personal application to register, usually at some centrally located office.

Voter-registration systems were used in the colonies and in some of the original thirteen states but were soon abolished in most jurisdictions because of citizens' objections to the annoyance. Their reestablishment, especially in states with large cities, where voting fraud was more prevalent, came largely in the 1860s, and as it became clear that voting fraud could occur in rural areas and small towns as well as in big cities, registration requirements were imposed in those places as well. Instituted first in the northern and eastern states, registration requirements spread to the western and southern ones.[45] One study of voter registration observed:

The historical trend of registration laws has been constantly to extend the application, and, as voting frauds occur, to make the system more and more stringent. The result is that registration in many states has become expensive, cumbersome, inconvenient to the voter, and not yet particularly effective in preventing frauds.[46]

In the past, registration laws usually required lengthy residence in the state, proof of residence, and registration only at a central office (such as a county courthouse or city hall), and the registration books had to be closed long before the date of the election. Once registered, an individual had only to vote at least once every few years (usually four or five) in order to remain registered, a system known as permanent registration. Some states used a periodic registration system, in which voters had to register periodically, whether they had voted or not. It is in part because of these requirements that the voter-turnout rate in the United States was and is one of the lowest among the developed democracies.[47]

Voter-registration systems are designed to prevent voting fraud. However, placing the burden of registration on the citizen means that the costs are greater for some citizens than for others. Many states require citizens to go to a central office in the city, township, or county to register. If the office is open only during working hours, many cannot leave their jobs to register. For many citizens, the value derived from voting participation is less than the costs imposed by the voter-registration system, and as a consequence many citizens are not registered and do not vote.[48]

Several schemes have been proposed to make registration easier. One is to shift from periodic to permanent registration, and this in fact has been implemented. In 1929, there were eighteen states with periodic registration in at least part of the state and twenty-nine with permanent registration in at least part of the state.[49] By 1988, almost all states had changed to permanent registration. Furthermore, twenty-five states now permit some form of registration by mail.[50] Under this system, forms are mailed to individuals upon their request, are made available in public places, such as libraries, or are distributed by various groups in the community. The citizen registers by completing the form and mailing it to the registration office. States using this system vary in the extent to which they check forms to prevent fraud.[51]

Four states have adopted election-day registration. In some of these states, citizens must register at a central office in the local jurisdiction before going to the polling place, while in others, a citizen may register at the polling place itself. In Wisconsin, for example, citizens may register at the polling place if they have proper identification or can be identified by a witness. The two states that were using election-day registration at the time of the 1976 election—Wisconsin and Minnesota—experienced an increase in voter turnout, whereas turnout declined that year in most other areas of the country.[52]

Election-day registration does have certain problems. One is that, if a large number of people attempt to register on election day, considerable delays may be experienced at the polling places. This occurred in Minnesota in 1976, where almost 23 percent of those voting registered on election day at a polling place.[53] A second problem is the danger of fraudulent registration; vigilant and vigorous enforcement of the law is also made more difficult when large numbers of people attempt to register on election day. One way of limiting fraud is to mail, after the election, a nonforwardable verification to the address of each election-day registrant. While that technique may limit future voting fraud by those who registered illegally on election day, the outcome of the election in which they have already voted is not affected.

An evaluation of election-day registration in Wisconsin after the 1976 election found such problems as long lines of voters angered by the delays, confusion caused by the process, voters who registered in the wrong districts, multiple registrations by some individuals, acceptance of inadequate proof of residence, and substantial additional costs of administration. Some of the same complaints were made about the Minnesota system. However, as noted, voter turnout did increase in both states, with substantial increases occurring in some of the larger cities.[54]

Several states facilitate voter registration by making registration materials available at agencies that have extensive contact with the public. For example, in Maryland applications for voter registration by mail (which may be used by citizens residing in any local jurisdiction) are available in public libraries, social welfare agencies, and motor vehicle administration offices.

One major problem with voter-registration procedures in the United States is that those who have recently moved must either reregister, if they have moved to a different jurisdiction, or file a change of address, if they have moved within the same city or county. Approximately 20 percent of the electorate have moved at least once within a two-year period, and approximately 45 percent have moved within a four-year period. The combination of registration procedures and the high mobility of the American population depresses voting turnout. Among those who have moved, the effects of moving on voting registration are greatest among those with lower levels of education, or who moved more recently, or who have lower levels of political interest.[55]

In most other democratic countries, the burden of voter registration is assumed by the government rather than by the individual. In one study of twenty-four democratic countries, only five required citizens to apply to be on the voting-registration list. In the others, either citizens are automatically registered because they are on some other government list, such as a residency list or list of taxpayers, or the government actively seeks to register its citizens by systematically canvassing every household.[56]

In Canada, which also has a federal system of government, the federal government does the work and bears the cost of registration. Two persons, one from each of the two parties winning the largest shares of the votes cast in that district in the preceding election, are appointed as enumerators in each election district. They go door to door in the constituency, listing the names of everyone in each household who is eligible to vote. If no one is at home after several calls at a household, a notice informing the residents of the enumerators' efforts to reach them is left, and a telephone number is given so that they can call and register themselves. A new list of registered voters is compiled before each election; the process takes six weeks. Elections can be called at any time in Canada, and this system ensures that an up-to-date list can be quickly drawn up.[57]

Great Britain uses registration by mail combined with a door-to-door system. The voting registrar is a government civil servant, not political-party activists as in Canada. The registrar is responsible for ensuring that each household is contacted, either personally or by mail. A new registration list is prepared once a year; it becomes effective about four months after the registration process begins. In several European countries, all residents are registered with an administrative agency in the area where they live, and lists of eligible voters are compiled from these residency lists. In Sweden, for example, the county governing boards are responsible for the residency lists; in West Germany, the police are. These lists are more up to date than the lists compiled under the British system.[58]

What are the effects of restrictive election laws and election-administration rules and procedures on voting turnout? Analysis of voter registration patterns in the 1972 presidential election suggests that just a few changes would have increased voting turnout by more than 9 percent. The change that would have produced the largest increase is eliminating the closing date for registration, but keeping registration offices open during the forty-hour work week, opening offices in the evenings and on Saturday, and permitting absentee registration for the sick, the disabled, and those away from the district on election day would also have helped.[59]

More elections for government offices are held in the United States than in most other democracies. One study of six states found that an average of eleven elections were held during a four-year period.[60] Only fourteen states schedule gubernatorial elections in presidential election years.[61] Some states elect their governors and state legislatures at a time when *no* federal-level officials—president, senator, or representative—are being elected. The increased use of primaries to nominate candidates for state and local offices and to select delegates to national nominating conventions adds to the number of elections. In one study, the average registered voter for whom records could be checked voted more than four times between 1972 and 1976.[62]

The use of run-off primaries in some states, designed to ensure that the party's nominees for office are selected by a majority rather than a plurality, may reduce voting turnout by increasing the total number of elections in which citizens are called upon to vote. Run-off primaries are held primarily in the South, where they developed when the southern states traditionally elected only Democrats to public office. Turnout declined from the initial primary to the run-off primary in three-fourths of all Democratic gubernatorial, senatorial, and congressional run-off elections held from 1956 to 1984. One explanation for this is the increasing presence of Republican opposition in the general-election contests; as Republican candidates' possibility of success in the general election increases, turnout in the Democratic party's run-off primaries decreases. Other factors that contribute to decreased turnout in run-off elections are a closed primary and a longer time period between the initial primary and the run-off primary.[63]

While turnout in some states has been dropping at the same time that the number of elections held in them has been rising, it has also dropped in states that do not hold more elections now than they did previously.[64] Studies comparing turnout among states over time, using state election data and voting-age population estimates, suggest that while the large number of elections held in the United States as compared to other democracies may decrease turnout in the nation as a whole, the differences in turnout among the states cannot be accounted for by differences in the number of elections they held.

The use of survey data permits controlling for the effects of personal characteristics—both sociodemographic and attitudinal—while testing for the effects of the presence or absence of contests for various types of offices. An examination of turnout using survey data collected in 1980 concludes that residents of states holding gubernatorial elections at the same time as presidential elections were slightly more likely to vote, with elections for governor being a greater stimulus for voter participation in the South than in northern states. Holding simultaneous senatorial elections had no effect on turnout among those surveyed in 1980. Presidential primaries had the effect of depressing general-election participation, especially among residents in those states that added presidential primaries after 1968.[65]

Many countries hold elections on a rest day, rather than on a workday as in the United States. Among twenty-seven democracies studied in 1980, thirteen schedule elections on a rest day and five schedule them for a two-day period covering both a workday and a rest day.[66] The number of hours the polls remain open, which may also affect turnout, varies in the United States from fifteen in New York to "at least four" in New Hampshire.[67] Other arrangements, such as the number of voting machines and the length of time one must wait to vote, can affect the turnout rate.

Changing voter-registration procedures to make it easier for those who have recently moved to register or reregister to vote would facilitate voting. One procedure for doing this would be to have the U.S. postal system provide change-of-address forms to voter-registration offices, thus allowing those who have moved to maintain eligibility to vote in elections for federal offices. This would require changed administrative procedures in some states, but would probably substantially increase voter turnout among persons who have recently moved.[68]

Finally, loosening rules for voting by mail could also increase turnout. A number of democracies make it easier than the United States does for citizens to vote by mail. Several also establish polling places in such institutions as hospitals and homes for the aged.[69]

Opportunities for Other Forms of Participation

The structure of the electoral system affects not only who votes but also who runs for office. States differ in the ways in which citizens qualify themselves to run for public office. Some states require candidates to pay a filing fee, and some also require candidates to obtain a specified number of signatures on a petition in order to run in a nominating election. The requirement of a large filing fee or a large number of signatures might discourage some citizens from running for office, although it is unlikely that a candidate who is able to attract the support of a significant number of other citizens would be discouraged by such requirements.

To eliminate frivolous candidacies, seven states require that candidates, to be eligible to enter a primary to seek their party's nomination for major statewide office, receive the support of some party body or set of officials. Usually this occurs at a state party convention. The proportion of convention delegates needed for this purpose is not high—as examples, 10 percent in Connecticut, 20 percent in Colorado, and 25 percent in New York. Endorsements, granted either formally by conventions or informally through party leaders' support, are also important in some states in winning a party nomination to run for state legislative office.[70]

Campaign-finance laws can operate to limit who can run for public office. The costs of political campaigns have increased more rapidly than the consumer price index. This has been in large part a consequence of the use of more expensive campaigning methods, such as polling and television advertising, and of professional campaign staff, such as advertising and survey-research experts, to do work that formerly either was not done at all or was done by volunteers. Meanwhile, campaign-finance laws at the national level and in many states have placed limits on who may contribute and how much may be contributed. These laws work to the advantage of candidates who are able to raise large sums of money in small amounts. For example, in a campaign for federal office in 1988, individual contributors were not permitted to donate more than $1,000, and political action committees (PACs) no more than $5,000 to any one candidate in an election contest. Thus, those candidates who could raise large sums in amounts of $1,000 or less, who attracted many PAC contributions, and who were independently wealthy and could make large contributions or loans to their own campaigns were in a more favorable position.

These changes in campaign-finance laws have stimulated the use of mass mail fund-raising solicitations by individual candidates, party organizations, and interest groups. A higher proportion of citizens report making political contributions now than ten years ago (see Table 1-2), and this, too, is a form of participation.

The federal government and the several layers of state and local governments create many potential contact points between citizens and public officials. In one survey, a little more than one-fourth of the respondents reported having expressed their views in writing to a government official.[71]

Much of the contacting of government officials that influences the content of public policy occurs through the activity of interest groups. For example, the interests of college students are represented through the U.S. Student Association and the Coalition of Independent College and University Students. In 1982, when the Reagan administration proposed changes in the programs providing grants and loans to college students, the association was an active member of a coalition of educational and other interest groups that successfully lobbied to prevent changes in the eligibility criteria as well as reductions in funding for the programs. Many thousands of such interest groups are active in lobbying the executive and legislative branches at all levels of government. They represent the interests of their members as perceived by the group's officers and staff, and their activities often go on without much awareness on the part of many of the group's members—who nonetheless help support these activities through their membership dues.[72]

Another arena for interest-group contacts with government is the judicial system. An interest group that believes an action by the executive or legislative branch is illegal or unconstitutional can seek to overturn it by a court decision. The number of government programs has increased substantially since the mid-1960s, and so has the use of the courts by interest groups pursuing a litigation strategy to obtain policy outcomes they have not been able to obtain from the executive or legislative branches.[73]

The multiple layers of government and their several branches provide many opportunities for citizen participation in public decision making. The policy process can be viewed as containing five stages: (1) enacting the law; (2) writing the regulations to put into effect the intent of the law; (3) developing the implementation procedures for carrying out the law and its accompanying regulations; (4) developing and putting into effect enforcement mechanisms to make sure that the policy is carried out and the relevant laws and regulations are enforced; and (5) creating and using evaluation procedures to determine if the law is having the desired effects. The potential for citizen involvement exists at each stage, but it varies with the nature of the policy area, the decision-making structure, the attitudes toward citizen participation of the agency of government involved, and the characteristics of the citizens. Consequently, citizen participation in the policy process varies greatly from one area to another.

The growth of the regulatory process, particularly at the federal level, has increased both the opportunity and the necessity for citizen contacts with the government. These contacts probably occur most often through the medium of business, labor, consumer, public-interest, and special-interest organizations, but some individual citizen contact also occurs. For example, citizens may comment on the regulations drafted to carry out a new law or on proposed revisions of existing regulations. State laws often mandate that public hearings be held before utility commissions can grant rate increases to electric, gas, water, telephone, and other companies. Participation by citizens' organizations in these hearings varies considerably among the states; in about half the states, these grass-roots organizations seem to meet with greater success when they focus on issues with low technical complexity and substantial political impact.[74]

Individual citizens' contacts with government often concern not the broad content of policy or the policy process but immediate personal problems. A citizen may complain to a local official or agency about such things as inadequate bus service, potholes in the streets, the need to improve street lighting, or the lack of an adequate science education program in the local high school. These contacts are a function of the need for a service, the demand for it, and the awareness of a governmental unit's ability and responsibility to deliver that service.[75] Some research suggests that service demand is in turn a function of socioeconomic status, with citizens of higher status being more likely to contact government agencies with demands for services than are citizens of lower socioeconomic status who have similar levels of service needs and awareness of service availability.[76] Other research indicates that contacting public agencies for service or information and filing complaints with them is more likely among those who are older and who have more positive evaluations of service-provision agencies; income appears not to be related to requests for service or information or the filing of complaints.[77] The extent of contacting by citizens of different socioeconomic status may vary with governmental structure: those of lower socioeconomic status are more likely to request service delivery in cities or counties that have a centralized complaint bureau.[78]

Citizen participation is sometimes required by the law that establishes a government program. Funding for many public works projects cannot be approved unless evidence is provided that the environmental impact of the project has been studied, an environmental impact statement prepared, and a public hearing held to obtain citizens' reactions to the project. If citizens residing in an area through which a new road is to be built decide that the laws governing the process under which the route of a new road is determined were not followed, they can, individually or as an organized group, petition to have the route changed by their state's transportation department, or they can file suit in court to try to block the construction. Citizens and citizen organizations have made increasing use of lawsuits, both to overturn laws and decisions and to compel the enforcement of laws that they believe the responsible government agency is not adequately enforcing.

Many government programs also require the establishment of citizen advisory boards, which may provide another forum for citizen input. Sometimes, however, these boards are composed largely of the representatives of specific interests associated with the program—either those who receive the program's services or those who are involved in delivering them. Citizen participation in the advisory process may lend increased legitimacy to a policy and its implementation, but if the resulting policy or its implementation is not in accord with the preferences of the citizen advisers, negative attitudes toward the agency and its policies are a likely consequence.[79]

Summary

Patterns of political participation can be significantly influenced by the structure of the government and by the laws and regulations enacted by the government. In the United States, the federal system of government creates many access points at which citizens can make their views known to government officials. One outgrowth of the federal system is the multiplicity of elections, offering more opportunities for electoral participation than occur in most other democratic nations. The federal Constitution reserves most aspects of election regulation and administration to the states, resulting in considerable variation in electoral laws. Many citizens have had problems in the past in gaining access to the ballot, but recent constitutional amendments and laws and court decisions at both state and federal levels have eliminated most of those problems.

Registration procedures, however, remain an electoral obstacle in many states. Unlike most other democratic nations, the United States requires citizens to present themselves in order to register to vote, rather than having government agents carry out voter registration with no initiative required from the citizens. That fact has significant effects on who participates in elections in the United States. Even in states using mail voter-registration systems, the citizen must obtain the appropriate form, fill it out, and mail it, a procedure that requires a degree of initiative and effort not called for in most other countries. The right to an absentee ballot also varies widely among the states and results in a reduced level of voting participation.

Other aspects of electoral and campaign activity are also affected by government laws and regulations. Patterns of campaign participation are influenced by the laws that govern eligibility to be a candidate for office and those that govern campaign finances. In most states, the patterns of other forms of campaign participation are affected by the regulation of political parties and their activities; these laws and regulations have tended to reduce the activity occurring through the political parties and to increase the activity occurring through candidates' own organizations.

The structure of government creates a pattern of access points for those who wish to influence government policy or to obtain specific benefits under existing government programs. Since early in their history, Americans have organized extensively into formal groups for the purpose of influencing the making, administering, and enforcing of government policy. During the past fifty years, the increased activity of government in many areas has stimulated a substantial growth in the number of interest groups represented in Washington.

Organized activity seeking to influence government policy has also expanded at the state and local levels. In part, this can be attributed to laws that require obtaining the views of citizens during the decision-making process; local government units often must hold public hearings before making final decisions on budgets, capital improvements, or the issuing of regulations. Both the division of government into three separate branches and the existence of several levels of government create numerous access points for citizens to use in influencing government activity.

Comparative studies of political participation reach differing conclusions about the relative importance of political and governmental institutions and of social and political culture in determining patterns of political participation. Research provides evidence that both contribute to the particular patterns found in the developed democracies. Different institutional and cultural patterns would undoubtedly produce different levels of participation in the United States.

NOTES

1. See David Butler, Howard R. Penniman, and Austin Ranney, "Introduction: Democratic and Non-Democratic Elections," in *Democracy at the Polls,* ed. David Butler, Howard R. Penniman, and Austin Ranney (Washington, D.C.: American Enterprise Institute, 1981), 1–6; and G. Bingham Powell, *Contemporary Democracies* (Cambridge: Harvard University Press, 1982).
2. The arguments in the Constitutional Convention on this subject are presented in Madison's "Notes on the Constitution"; see Max Farrand (ed.), *The Records of the Federal Convention of 1787,* 3 vols. (New Haven: Yale University Press, 1911).
3. See Kirk Harold Porter, *A History of Suffrage in the United States* (New York: AMS Press, 1971), chap. 1; and Dudley O. McGovney, *The American Suffrage Medley* (Chicago: University of Chicago Press, 1949), chap. 2.
4. The amount required varied with the nature of the state's economy. In New England, few farms were as large as 50 acres, while in the South most farms were at least that large. See Porter, *History of Suffrage,* 7–14.

5. Ibid., chaps. 2, 3, and 4.
6. Charles E. Johnson, Jr., *Nonvoting Americans*, Bureau of the Census Current Population Reports, series P-23, no. 102 (Washington, D.C.: Government Printing Office, 1980), 2, table A.
7. Eleanor Flexner, *Century of Struggle* (Cambridge: Harvard University Press, 1959), 15.
8. Ibid.
9. Ibid., 164.
10. Ibid., chap. 3.
11. Ibid., chap. 5.
12. Ibid., 74–77.
13. Barbara Sinclair Deckard, *The Women's Movement*, 3d ed. (New York: Harper and Row, 1983), 255–264; and Nancy McGlen and Karen O'Connor, *Women's Rights: The Struggle for Equality in the Nineteenth and Twentieth Centuries* (New York: Praeger, 1983), 44–53.
14. John J. Stucker, "Women as Voters: Their Maturation as Political Persons in American Society," in *A Portrait of Marginality*, ed. M. Githens and J. L. Prestage (New York: David McKay, 1977), 268.
15. Ibid., 269–270.
16. Deckard, *Women's Movement*, 281; Flexner, *Century of Struggle*, chap. 17; and McGlen and O'Connor, *Women's Rights*, 53–63.
17. Flexner, *Century of Struggle*, chap. 22.
18. Richard P. Claude, *The Supreme Court and the Electoral Process* (Baltimore: Johns Hopkins University Press, 1970), 53–63.
19. For a discussion of the use of the poll tax to exclude black voters in the South, see V. O. Key, Jr., *Southern Politics* (New York: Vintage, 1949), chap. 27.
20. *Guinn v. United States*, 238 U.S. 347 (1915); and *Lane v. Wilson*, 307 U.S. 263 (1939). For a discussion of these cases, see Claude, *Supreme Court*, 74. For a discussion of the origins and use of the "grandfather clause," see Key, *Southern Politics*, 535–539.
21. *Nixon v. Herndon*, 273 U.S. 536 (1927).
22. *Nixon v. Condon*, 286 U.S. 73 (1932).
23. *U.S. v. Classic*, 313 U.S. 299 (1941); and *Smith v. Allwright*, 321 U.S. 659 (1944).
24. David M. Chalmers, *Hooded Americanism: The First Century of the Ku Klux Klan, 1865–1965*, 2d ed. (New York: Franklin Watts, 1981); Arnold S. Rice, *The Ku Klux Klan in Politics*, Southern Literature and History Series, no. 65 (Brooklyn: Haskell Booksellers, 1972); and William Gillette, *Retreat from Reconstruction, 1869–1879* (Baton Rouge: Louisiana State University Press, 1979), 25–28, 52–55.
25. See Commission on Civil Rights, *Political Participation* (Washington, D.C.: Government Printing Office, 1968), part III, chap. 7.
26. Sections 3 and 11b, Voting Rights Act of 1965, 79 Stat. 437, 42 U.S.C. 1973.
27. For a discussion of the rule and its repeal, see Austin Ranney, *Curing the Mischiefs of Faction* (Berkeley and Los Angeles: University of California Press, 1975), 71, 75–76.
28. For the contents of this and the Civil Rights Law of 1957, see House Committee on the Judiciary, *Civil Rights Acts of 1957, 1960, 1964, 1968 (As Amended through the 93rd Congress, First Session)*, 93d Cong., 1st sess., 1974.
29. This act also required that election records, voter registration documents, and poll-tax records be kept for twenty-two months, and upon request be provided to the attorney general.
30. For a brief history of the extensions, see "Voting Rights Act Extension Cleared for President Reagan," *Congressional Quarterly Weekly Report*, June 26, 1982, 1503.

31. Sidney Verba, Norman H. Nie, and Jae-on Kim, *Participation and Political Equality* (Cambridge: Cambridge University Press, 1978).
32. M. Margaret Conway, "Political Participation in Midterm Congressional Elections: Attitudinal and Social Characteristics during the 1970s," *American Politics Quarterly* 9 (1981): 229–232; Stephen D. Shaffer, "A Multivariate Explanation of Decreasing Turnout in Presidential Elections, 1960–1976," *American Journal of Political Science* 25 (1981): 68–95; and Howard L. Reiter, "Why Is Turnout Down?," *Public Opinion Quarterly* 43 (1979): 297–311.
33. Raymond E. Wolfinger and Steven J. Rosenstone, *Who Votes?* (New Haven: Yale University Press, 1980), 18. See also Gabriel A. Almond and Sidney Verba, *The Civic Culture: Political Attitudes and Democracy in Five Nations* (Boston: Little, Brown, 1965), 315–321; and Robert E. Lane, *Political Life* (Glencoe, Ill.: Free Press, 1959), chap. 16.
34. G. Bingham Powell, "American Voting Behavior in Comparative Perspective," *American Political Science Review* 80 (March 1986): 23.
35. Ibid., 19, table 1.
36. Ibid., 33–37.
37. Robert W. Jackman, "Political Institutions and Voter Turnout in the Industrial Democracies," *American Political Science Review* 81 (June 1987): 405–423.
38. For a discussion of the origins and aims of voter-registration systems, see Joseph P. Harris, *Registration of Voters in the United States* (Washington, D.C.: Brookings Institution, 1929).
39. See *Oregon v. Mitchell, Texas v. Mitchell, United States v. Idaho, United States v. Arizona,* 400 U.S. 112 (1970); *Dunn v. Blumstein,* 405 U.S. 330 (1972); *Marston v. Lewis,* 410 U.S. 679 (1973); *Burns v. Fortson,* 410 U.S. 686 (1973).
40. In 1950, the requirement for residency in the state was six months in eleven states, one year or twelve months in thirty-four, and two years in five. Council of Governments, *Book of the States, 1950–1951* (Chicago: Council of Governments, 1950).
41. Robert Erikson, "Why Do People Vote? Because They Are Registered," *American Politics Quarterly* 9 (1981): 259–276.
42. U.S. Bureau of the Census, *Statistical Abstract of the United States, 1984* (Washington, D.C.: Government Printing Office, 1983), 265, table 440.
43. U.S. Bureau of the Census, "Voting and Registration in the Election of November, 1988," Current Population Surveys, Series P-20, No. 435 (February 1989).
44. Harris, *Registration,* 67.
45. Ibid., 72–89.
46. Ibid., 89.
47. Ivor Crewe, "Electoral Participation," in *Democracy at the Polls,* ed. Butler, Penniman, and Ranney, 232–239.
48. Francis Fox Piven and Richard A. Cloward, "Government Statistics and Conflicting Explanations of Nonvoting," *PS* 22 (September 1989): 580–588.
49. Harris, *Registration,* 97–99. One state had no registration system at the time.
50. Council of State Governments, *Book of the States 1982–1983,* 105, table 5.
51. For a discussion of the operations of such a system in two states, see Richard Smolka, *Registering Voters by Mail* (Washington, D.C.: American Enterprise Institute, 1975).
52. Richard Smolka, *Election Day Registration* (Washington, D.C.: American Enterprise Institute, 1977), 45.
53. Ibid., 26.
54. Ibid., 23–26, 40–45.
55. Peverill Squire, Raymond E. Wolfinger, and David P. Glass, "Residential Mobility and Voter Turnout," *American Political Science Review* 81 (March 1987): 45–65.

56. Interparliamentary Union, *Parliaments of the World* (New York: Macmillan, 1976). See also Crewe, "Electoral Participation," 240–250.
57. William Crotty, *Political Reform and the American Experiment* (New York: Crowell, 1977), 76–78.
58. Ibid., 74–75.
59. Wolfinger and Rosenstone, *Who Votes?*, 72–78.
60. Richard Boyd, "Decline of U.S. Voter Turnout," *American Politics Quarterly* 9 (1981): 145.
61. Ibid., 140.
62. Ibid., 147.
63. Stephen G. Wright, "Voter Turnout in Runoff Elections," *Journal of Politics* 51 (May 1989): 385–397.
64. Jeffrey Cohen, "Change in Election Calendars and Turnout Decline," *American Politics Quarterly* 10 (1982): 246–254.
65. Richard W. Boyd, "Election Calendars and Voter Turnout," *American Politics Quarterly* 14 (January–April 1986): 89–104.
66. Crewe, "Electoral Participation," 242–247, table 10.4.
67. Council of State Governments, *Book of the States 1980–1981*, 68–69, table 6.
68. See Squire, Wolfinger, and Glass, "Residential Mobility," 57–58.
69. Crewe, "Electoral Participation," 242–247, table 10.4. An objection to the use of absentee ballots is that they may contribute to problems of fraud and voter intimidation. For example, during the 1960s, in one small county in a midwestern state, more persons appeared to have voted than actually lived in the county according to the census data, and many of the votes had been cast on absentee ballots.
70. Malcolm E. Jewell and David M. Olson, *American State Political Parties and Elections*, rev. ed. (Homewood, Ill.: Dorsey, 1982), 111–120.
71. Warren E. Miller and Santa A. Traugott, *American National Election Studies Data Sourcebook, 1952–1986* (Cambridge: Harvard University Press, 1989), 295, table 5.6.
72. For a discussion of the changing patterns of interest-group politics, see Allan J. Cigler and Burdett A. Loomis, "Introduction: The Changing Nature of Interest Group Politics," in *Interest Group Politics*, ed. Allan J. Cigler and Burdett A. Loomis, 2d ed. (Washington, D.C.: CQ Press, 1986), 1–27.
73. For a discussion of the litigation strategies of interest groups, see Stephen L. Wasby, "Interest Groups in Court: Race Relations Litigation," in *Interest Group Politics*, ed. Cigler and Loomis, 251–270; Karen O'Connor, *Women's Organizations' Use of the Courts* (Lexington, Mass.: Lexington Books, 1970); and Karen O'Connor and Lee Epstein, "The Rise of Conservative Interest Group Litigation," *Journal of Politics* 45 (1983): 479–489.
74. William T. Gormley, Jr., "Policy, Politics, and Public Utility Regulation," *American Journal of Political Science* 27 (1983): 86–105.
75. Bryan D. Jones, Saadia R. Greenberg, Clifford Kaufman, and Joseph Drew, "Bureaucratic Response to Citizen-Initiated Contacts: Environmental Enforcement in Detroit," *American Political Science Review* 71 (1977): 148–165.
76. Elaine B. Sharp, "Citizen-Initiated Contacting of Government Officials and Socio-economic Status: Determining the Relationship and Accounting for It," *American Political Science Review* 76 (1982): 109–115; and Elaine B. Sharp, "Citizen Demand in the Urban Context," *American Journal of Political Science* 28 (1984): 654–670.
77. Rodney E. Hero, "Explaining Citizen-Initiated Contacting of Government Officials: Socioeconomic Status, Perceived Need, or Something Else?" *Social Science Quarterly* 67 (1986): 626–635.
78. Arnold Vedlitz, James A. Dyer, and Roger Durand, "Citizen Contacts with Local Governments: A Comparative View," *American Journal of Political Science* 24 (1980): 50–67.

79. J. Vincent Buck, "The Impact of Citizen Participation Programs and Policy Decisions on Participants' Opinions," *Western Political Quarterly* 37 (1984): 468–482; and Daniel Maxmanian and Jeanne Nienaber, *Can Organizations Change? Environmental Protection, Citizen Participation, and the Corps of Engineers* (Washington, D.C.: Brookings Institution, 1979).

Chapter 6

The Rationality of Political Participation

The question has often been raised as to whether a rational person participates in politics at all. A rational person may be defined as one "who moves toward his goals in a way which, to the best of his knowledge, uses the least possible input of scarce resources per unit of valued output."[1] To be rational, then, is to be efficient in the use of resources to obtain one's goals.[2] A rational person is an individual who considers all alternatives, arrives at a "transitive preference ordering" among them, and chooses the one most preferred.[3] (*Transitive* means that if *A* is preferred to *B*, and *B* is preferred to *C*, then *A* is preferred to *C*.) The classic definition in rational-choice theory, an approach to the study of human behavior developed first in economics, is that a rational person "maximizes expected utility."[4]

A more elaborate and restrictive conception describes the steps in the process of rational choice as "(1) the individual evaluates alternatives in his environment on the basis of his preferences among them; (2) his preference ordering is consistent and transitive; (3) he always chooses the preferred alternative." This conception is subject to the restrictions that the individual performs the evaluation of alternatives in terms of expected values and does not give direct consideration to changes in the happiness of others caused by his actions; that is, "the individual does not value the utility of others as an end in itself." It also assumes that individuals operate in terms of a particular set of roles and that the actions associated with one specified role are more important than the actions associated with any other role. Furthermore, "the sources of the benefits and costs which accrue to the individual from the specified role are differentiated from other aspects of the environment." Finally, it is also assumed that individuals have access to a substantial amount of information when alternatives are evaluated, but that predictions about the behavior of others are made with some degree of uncertainty.[5]

It is explicit in this conception (and implicit in other conceptions) that rational individuals do not give direct consideration to changes in the happiness of others as a consequence of their choices, but it can be argued that rationality does not preclude individuals from being motivated by altruistic values.[6] Several scholars have tried to incorporate various forms of motivation other than narrow self-interest into their formulation of the calculus of rational choice. For example, one analysis of voting participation included a term that encompassed such considerations as the satisfactions gained from affirming allegiance to the political system, expressing a partisan preference, deciding how to vote, and conforming to the democratic norms through the act of voting.[7] In his formulation of vote choice, Downs included a term representing "long-run participation value"—the value derived from the survival of the political system through citizens' participation in key political processes such as voting.[8] It could be argued, however, that this "long-run participation value" term has "extra-rational" connotations.

If to be rational is to be efficient in allocating scarce resources in seeking to obtain one's goals, then one must ask whether political participation is an efficient use of resources. What can one try to obtain through political participation? The answer to that question can be divided into two parts, political outcomes and personal outcomes. Political outcomes would be the victory of a candidate or party in an election, the passage or defeat of a referendum or initiative, the defeat or enactment of a particular law, the enforcement of a law or policy through the drafting of particular regulations or their implementation, or the appointment of a particular person to public office. Personal outcomes have frequently been ignored, but they can be important: Individuals may enjoy participation in politics for its own sake, just as some individuals enjoy sailing or playing softball or tennis. They may participate for the social contacts or for the sense of contribution to the future success of a cause in which they believe.

Voting as Rational Behavior

If the rationality of voting were to be based on the probability that one's vote would determine the outcome of the election, most persons would conclude that this probability is so small that voting would not be an efficient use of resources unless it was costless. Nevertheless, a majority of the electorate does vote in presidential elections. For many citizens, the benefits of voting appear to outweigh its costs. These costs of voting include gathering the information necessary to make a choice; registering to vote, which may involve merely filling out a postcard and putting it in the mail or the more costly act of traveling to the county or city courthouse; and going to the polls, which may require taking time off from work or may involve inconvenience costs, such as getting to the polls early to vote before going to work or finding and paying a baby sitter.

Downs has set forth these propositions:

1. When voting is costless, every citizen who is indifferent abstains, and every citizen who has any preference whatsoever votes.

2. If voting is costly, it is rational for some indifferent citizens to vote and for some citizens with preferences to abstain.

3. When voting costs exist, small changes in their size may radically alter the distribution of political power.

4. The costs of voting act to disenfranchise low-income citizens relative to high-income citizens.

5. It is sometimes rational for citizens to vote even when their short-run costs exceed their short-run returns, because social responsibility produces a long-run return.[9]

Riker and Ordeshook have embodied the evaluative decision of whether or not to vote in a formula,

$$R = PB - C + D$$

where

R is the expected utility an individual derives from voting minus the expected utility of abstaining;

P is the probability that the individual's vote will make a difference in the outcome of the election;

B is the benefit an individual receives if his or her preferred candidate or party wins the election;

C is the cost of voting; and

D is the social satisfaction derived from voting, which includes the long-run participation value, compliance with the norm that the good citizen always votes, the satisfaction derived from the maintenance and survival of the political system, and the enjoyment derived from involvement in the political process.[10]

Since the value of P is generally very small—say, 1/10,000—it is apparent that D, the social satisfaction derived from voting, must be very large if citizens are to be motivated to vote.[11] It would also help if C were kept as small as possible. That can be achieved individually by using easy cues for how to vote, such as reliance on party identification or on an already known candidate, or collectively, by instituting easy registration procedures, having registration done by the government rather than relying on citizen initiative, giving time off from work to vote or holding the election on a nonwork day or on a national holiday, and providing easily accessible polling places (see Chapter 5).

Several additional terms have been suggested for the above equation. One is "minimax regret," which is based on the assumption that voters seek to minimize their maximum regret at what the outcome would be if they did not vote. Suppose an individual did not vote and did not encourage her friends to vote, and her favorite candidate lost in a very close election; she would have a maximum level of regret. Voters vote and encourage their friends to vote in order to avoid that experience.[12]

It has also been argued that citizens vote out of an ethical imperative, a belief that they have a moral obligation to vote.

This belief is more widely held than acted upon, however; far more citizens state in surveys of public opinion that a good citizen should vote than actually turn out to vote in elections.[13] Another explanation is that, in deciding whether to vote, citizens take into account not merely the impact of their one vote but also the impact of the votes of people who have certain similar characteristics or who think as they do.[14] For example, rather than thinking only about the effect of one vote in electing people to office who will be vigilant in protecting the environment, a citizen may consider what the effect will be if many other people who care about environmental quality cast their votes on the basis of the candidates' past records on environmental issues and their promises for future action. The group impact could be considerable if voters make known that they care about an issue and that their vote choice will be significantly influenced by a particular policy or set of policy concerns.

A distinction can be made between *consumption benefits,* which are those deriving from the performance of the act itself—such as the pleasure derived from voting against candidates one dislikes or the approval one gets from politically interested friends because one has voted—and *investment rewards,* which are dependent upon the outcome of the election.

If the leaders of a group can increase turnout among their members and use the potential increased turnout as a bargaining tool to persuade a candidate to adopt policies more favorable to the group or to maintain already favorable policies, then the leaders have policy benefits with which to reward group members. If the result of the negotiations is to move the candidate's policy position closer to the group's preferred position, then the leaders have increased the policy goods available, which can then either be distributed to members or used in part to reward the leaders—for example, with new positions administering the programs that result. The rewards may also be altruistic, as when those who advocate programs to improve the quality of the environment know that they have contributed to the attainment of that goal. Candidates benefit from negotiating with group leaders by increasing either the probability that they will win or the margin of their victory.[15] The probability that they will negotiate for additional group support would be expected to decrease with the size of their expected victory margin.

Another approach to rationality in voting is to examine the fit between a citizen's issue positions and the perceived issue positions of the candidates seeking office. If one candidate is close to the citizen's issue preferences and the other candidate is quite far from them, the citizen would have a clear issue-difference basis for voting. Assuming that at least one of these issues is important to the citizen, that person would be more likely to vote in the election. However, the candidates may be perceived as equally close to the citizen's own issue positions, in which case there are no perceived issue differences between them. Thus, there would be no stimulus for voting turnout based on issues. Alternatively, the candidates may be perceived as being equally distant from the citizen's issue positions; this perceived distance from the candidates could also lead to nonvoting among those citizens who care about issue differences among candidates. John Zipp tested this formulation of the vote-decision process, using data collected during the 1968, 1972, 1976, and 1980 presidential elections. Lack of difference between candidates' issue positions was important in accounting for nonvoting in 1972, 1976, and 1980, although the significant issues varied. Alienation from the candidates on the basis of the distance of their issue positions from those of the citizen reduced voting turnout in 1968, 1972, and 1976, but again the issues that contributed to alienation varied across elections.[16]

The Substitutability of Other Activities

Experimental studies demonstrate that individuals who become aware of the low probability that their vote will make a difference in an election's outcome become more negative toward elections.[17] If that is the case, then citizens may choose to participate in other ways, either in addition to or as a substitute for voting. Other forms of participation could be viewed as more cost effective; for example, writing a letter to an elected official urging support for a particular policy, such as keeping a neighborhood elementary school open, may be perceived by the citizen

TABLE 6-1

Participation in Political Activities by Voters and Nonvoters, 1976

(percent reporting each type of activity)

	Voters	Nonvoters
Nationally oriented activities		
Wrote letter to editor	4.7	2.0
Worked with others	11.0	3.9
Wrote to representative or other national leader	21.6	13.1
Signed petition	13.0	7.3
Participated in sit-in, demonstration, or protest	1.7	1.3
Locally oriented activities		
Attended school board or city council meeting	25.2	15.7
Wrote letter to editor	6.3	3.2
Worked with others	26.0	18.0
Spoke or wrote to official	23.9	14.5
Signed petition	25.3	18.1
Participated in sit-in, demonstration, or protest	3.2	0.9
N	(1,087)	(689)

SOURCE: American National Election Studies, Center for Political Studies, University of Michigan.

as a more efficient way of obtaining the desired outcome—if the citizen can assume that the elected official is both attentive and responsive to citizen preferences. Or citizens could resort to more aggressive forms of participation, such as rent strikes, protest marches and demonstrations, occupation of buildings, or acts of violence, in the belief that these are more likely to be effective.

The 1976 American National Election Study, conducted by the Center for Political Studies of the University of Michigan, includes data that can be used to examine the extent to which individuals who do not vote engage in other forms of political activity. The individuals surveyed were asked whether they had voted that year and whether they had engaged in the previous two or three years in a number of other activities oriented toward national problems and issues and toward local government and politics.[18] Patterns of performance can also be examined in the light of the respondents' reported frequency of voting in past presidential elections in which they were eligible to vote.

Tables 6-1 and 6-2 indicate that in 1976, voters were more likely than nonvoters to engage in all forms of national and local political activity, regardless of whether it consisted of contacting the media or elected officials, community work, or protest. Participation in 1976 may have been constrained by the unusual context of the election, which followed the Watergate scandal and the prior resignations from office of both the president and the vice-president elected in 1972. Examining participation in national and local political activity by reported frequency of voting in past elections, and not just the 1976 election, provides one way of removing some of the effects of the unusual context. Table 6-2 indicates that habitual voters are more likely to engage

TABLE 6-2

Participation in Political Activities by Frequency of Voting in Past Presidential Elections, 1976

(percent reporting each type of activity)

	Frequency of voting in past presidential elections			
	All	Most	Some	None
Nationally oriented activities				
Wrote letter to editor	6.4	1.5	1.4	0
Worked with others	13.5	6.2	5.7	0.5
Wrote to representative or other national leader	27.6	13.6	8.9	6.8
Signed petition	16.1	9.4	3.2	4.8
Participated in sit-in, demonstration, or protest	2.6	0.5	1.1	0.5
Locally oriented activities				
Attended school board or city council meeting	28.8	20.6	9.6	13.0
Wrote letter to local editor	8.1	4.0	2.8	1.0
Worked with others	29.8	23.8	11.0	13.5
Spoke or wrote to official	27.8	18.9	14.5	8.2
Signed petition	31.7	19.6	6.0	17.9
Participated in sit-in, demonstration, or protest	3.2	1.5	1.1	1.0
N	(862)	(403)	(282)	(207)

SOURCE: American National Election Studies, Center for Political Studies, University of Michigan.

TABLE 6-3

Participation in Campaign Activities by Voters and Nonvoters,
1976 and 1988

(percent reporting each type of activity)

	1976		1988	
	Voters	Nonvoters	Voters	Nonvoters
Tried to persuade others	43.1	23.4	35.8	8.8
Attended political meetings	7.6	3.2	9.4	1.4
Worked for party or candidate	6.1	1.5	4.5	.3
Wore campaign button/sticker	9.2	3.2	11.3	1.9
Gave money	12.0	1.5	11.9	1.0
N	(1,087)	(689)	(1,230)	(800)

SOURCE: American National Election Studies, Center for Political Studies, University of Michigan.

in all forms of national and local political activity than are those who report infrequent voting in presidential elections. However, those who in 1976 claimed never to have voted in a presidential election did claim to engage in some forms of political action more frequently than did infrequent voters. The participation gap was larger in the locally than in the nationally oriented activities.

Other questions included in the American National Election Studies asked if the citizen had been involved in several types of activities related to the campaigns. Voters' and nonvoters' frequency of performing these campaign activities can be compared. If a substitution effect is occurring, we would expect nonvoters to be engaging in campaign activities at a relatively high level. Table 6-3 shows that, as would be expected, those who vote are more likely to have engaged in various forms of campaign activity than nonvoters. However, 23 percent of the nonvoters did claim to have attempted to persuade someone how to vote in the 1976 election. How is this to be explained? Why should people who don't vote themselves try to persuade others how to vote? One explanation relates to the time frame, or rather the lack of it, in the question. Respondents were asked about their activities "during the campaign," and it is not clear how they interpreted that phrase. Persuasion efforts could have occurred during the nominating process, with citizens trying to persuade others how to vote in the primary or caucus; and then, if their preferred candidate did not get the nomination, they did not vote in the general election. Another possibility is that nonvoters tried to persuade others not to vote. In contrast to the 23.4 percent who reported trying to persuade others how to vote in 1976, only 8.8 percent reported engaging in that activity in 1988. Reported participation in all other forms of campaign activity was also lower in 1988 than in 1976.

In other types of campaign-related participation, nonvoters were less likely to report having been approached by others in persuasion efforts than were voters. Nonvoters' reported participation in other forms of campaign-related activity is much smaller than that reported by voters.

Two summary indices were constructed from the 1976 response data: participation in locally oriented political activities during the previous two or three years, and participation in nationally oriented political activities during the previous two or three years. A little less than half the respondents whose voting participation could be checked reported engaging in at least one type of locally oriented activity in 1976 (see Table 6-4). In contrast, only about one-quarter performed any type of nationally oriented activity. Similarly, almost 14 percent said they had been involved in three or more types of local activity, but less than 4 percent had engaged in that many nationally oriented activities. Nonvoters scored lower than voters on both indices, but when nonvoters did participate, it was more likely to be in local activities than in national ones.

The analysis of the relative frequencies of participating in campaigns and in nationally and locally oriented political activities suggests that although nonvoters are not entirely nonparticipants in politics, they tend to engage in these forms of political activity less often than do voters. Reported participation in campaign activities by nonvoters has decreased, with only 11 percent reporting campaign activity in 1988 compared with 27 percent in 1976 (see Table 6-5). Data on national and local political activism are not available for 1988 or any other years since 1976. It is true that some nonvoters report a high frequency of engaging in political activities other than voting, but they represent a very

TABLE 6-4

Indices of Political Activity by Voters and
Nonvoters, 1976

(in percent)

	Total	Voters	Nonvoters
Locally oriented activity			
0	52.6	47.7	60.5
1	21.9	22.8	20.5
2	11.8	12.4	10.9
3	8.1	10.0	5.1
4	3.3	4.0	2.3
5	2.2	3.1	.7
Nationally oriented activity			
0	73.9	69.1	81.4
1	15.0	17.2	11.6
2	7.4	8.7	5.4
3	2.2	2.9	1.2
4	1.2	1.7	.4
5	.2	.4	0
N	(1,776)	(1,087)	(689)

SOURCE: American National Election Studies, Center for Political Studies, University of Michigan.

Note: o = participated in none of the activities listed in Table 6-1 (locally and nationally oriented activities) or 6-3 (campaign activity); 5 = participated in all of them. (Factor analyses resulted in dropping participation in sit-in, demonstration, or protest from the index of locally oriented activities. "Others tried to persuade them" is not included in the index of campaign activity.)

small proportion of nonvoters. It appears that, for the most part, citizens do not perceive other forms of political activity as an appropriate substitute for voting—though that does not in itself refute the rationality of such activity.

The Rationality of Group Formation and Maintenance

An inquiry into the rationality of political activity must also consider why people join together to seek to obtain what economists call "collective goods." A collective good is distinguished by two characteristics: indivisibility of benefit, and jointness of supply. *Indivisibility of benefit* means that it is available for use by all citizens, even if they have not contributed to its provision. A public highway is one example: Anyone can use it, whether or not they paid a share of the taxes with which it was constructed. *Jointness of supply* means that one person's use of the good does not replace the amount available to others. A frequently cited good in joint supply is air, and examples of goods in joint supply that are provided by the government are fire protection and police protection.[19] Collective goods are subject to "crowding," if so many people try to use them that the enjoyment of them is limited. For example, a city highway may become so clogged by traffic during rush hours that the vehicles move very slowly, or so many people may go to a public park on a pleasant summer weekend that all of them enjoy it less than they would otherwise. Collective goods may also be optional; that is, people can exclude themselves from the use of the good. For example, publicly funded education through grade twelve is a collective good in the United States, but individuals may withdraw from school before completing the twelfth grade if they have reached the age designated by state law beyond which school attendance is no longer mandatory. Furthermore, some public-education facilities are also exclusionary; institutions of higher education may have admissions requirements, such as minimum grade-point average or entrance-examination scores. The government may also supply collective goods through regulation of private actions, as in the case of the air traffic control system.

TABLE 6-5

Indices of Campaign Activity, 1976 and 1988

(in percent)

	1976			1988		
	Voters	Nonvoters	Total	Voters	Nonvoters	Total
0	51.1	73.3	60.0	54.2	89.4	68.1
1	30.5	20.3	26.1	29.5	8.8	21.3
2	11.9	3.6	8.8	9.1	1.4	6.1
3	3.3	2.3	3.0	4.1	.4	2.6
4	1.9	.4	1.3	2.4	.1	1.5
5	1.2	0	.9	.7	0	.4
N	(1,087)	(689)	(1,776)	(1,230)	(800)	(2,030)

SOURCE: American National Election Studies, Center for Political Studies, University of Michigan.

If individuals are expected to be utility maximizers, and if each is concerned with maximizing only his or her interests and not the interests of others, as rational choice theory generally assumes, then why would any individual contribute to obtaining a collective good? It would be rational to do so only if the benefit derived exceeds the cost and if the individual's contribution is crucial for obtaining it. But why should an individual contribute to the construction of, say, a new park, when others will give sufficient money for its construction and it will be open to all whether or not they have contributed?

Some scholars argue that, indeed, citizens will not contribute to the provision of a collective good unless they are coerced. One form of such coercion is the mandatory payment of taxes, with the tax revenues being used to provide such collective goods as fire and police protection, schools, hospitals, and streets and highways. Alternatively, individuals may be induced to contribute to the provision of a collective good by offering goods or services only to those who do contribute. For example, many groups that lobby the government to obtain collective goods beneficial to their members use low-cost insurance, reduced rates for travel, and free publications as inducements for people to become and remain members of the group. These members contribute either directly (through their activities) or indirectly (by belonging and hence adding to the numerical strength of the group) to persuading the government to provide the desired collective good, which could be a special tax deduction or reduced government regulation of their businesses.[20]

In Olson's theory of collective action, emphasis is placed upon the impossibility of excluding individuals who have not contributed to the supply of a collective good from enjoying its use. This is usually referred to as the "free rider" problem. Olson hypothesizes that a contribution to collective action will occur if the benefits accruing to an individual as a result of the collective action exceed the individual's costs. If benefits exceed costs for a number of individuals, Olson argues, a group will form; in his terms, the group is "privileged." If benefits do not exceed costs, the group is "latent," and unless incentives are offered to stimulate individual contributions to the provision of the collective good, collective action will not occur. Olson also posits a relationship between group size and privilege or latency, arguing that large groups may fail to supply a collective good where small groups may succeed. The larger the group, the less benefit any one member receives from the increment in the collective good provided through his contribution; the implication is that, in a large group, the benefit derived by the individual will be less than the cost of the increment.[21] But there is no necessary relationship between group size and group latency. Rather, what is crucial is the necessary size of any *subgroup* that will benefit from the provision of the collective good, this size being a function of the cost of the good and its benefit to the members of the subgroup.[22] When a subgroup has formed, it may act on behalf of the entire group.

Evidence from both experimental and field studies demonstrates that Olson's theory does not adequately account for collective behavior. Experimental studies, including some that allowed for discussion among participants and some that did not, show patterns of contribution to collective action that are contrary to what would be predicted by the theory.[23] And outside the experimental laboratory, it is apparent that many citizens contribute to collective action without coercion or incentives. Indeed, it appears that there has been a considerable increase in the number, activity, and impact of groups—some of them quite large—seeking to influence the public agenda or policy outcomes.[24] These groups seek not only the provision of collective goods but also the elimination of "collective bads."[25] How are these phenomena to be explained?

One answer that has been suggested emphasizes the role of "entrepreneurs" in organizing and maintaining groups. A related hypothesis is that individuals are by nature group oriented, with narrow self-interest being a learned behavior and with individuals varying in the types of activities in which narrow self-interest guides behavior. Another is that "implicit contract by coordination" is the major mechanism by which organizations aimed at obtaining collective goods arise. A third suggests that individuals have not one but two utility functions, the satisfaction of self-interest and the satisfaction of group interest, and they distribute their resources between the two. A fourth argument is that individuals derive utility from the very act of seeking collective goods; in other words, the supposed cost should actually be treated as a benefit.

The first of these suggested answers portrays political leaders as entrepreneurs who stimulate organizational formation by promising to provide group members either with desired values, such as services, which could function as incentives, or with collective goods.[26] The entrepreneur recruits members, structures the organization to provide benefits to them, and manages the organization's internal operations and its external relations with rival organizations, cooperating organizations, and political and administrative decision makers. The entrepreneur must ensure that costs and benefits are such that both members and the entrepreneur experience a net gain through the activities of the organization.[27] In addition to explicitly selective incentives, communication through both direct and indirect contacts can be an incentive as well as an organizational tool. More important, the entrepreneur can promote group membership through emphasis on the organization's and the entrepreneur's roles in the creation and maintenance of collective goods. Administration of collective goods through the entrepreneur's activities can become an incentive to join in organized activity and to contribute to obtaining the collective good.[28]

Much of the research on group formation and activity assumes a narrow economic self-interest as the basis on which cost-benefit calculations and decisions to contribute or not to contribute to group activity are made. Such an assumption simplifies the modeling of decision processes, but it does not reflect the realities of group formation and activity. Contributions to group activity may be motivated by one or more of many different kinds of incentives, both tangible and intangible.[29] The pursuit of collective goods by some of the newer single-issue groups appears to be based on their members' fervent belief in a cause. Two types of payoffs from contributions to an effort to obtain noneconomic collective goods, such as clean air or legalization of abortion, are possible. One is the enactment and enforcement of the policy itself; the second is the benefit the citizen derives from the activity of trying to obtain the collective good—that is, from political participation itself. These payoffs to group members can be fostered by the activities of the entrepreneur through management of group activities and communications.

Individuals can use several strategies to cope with the possibility that the return from their contributions to collective action may be quite small. One is the previously mentioned assessment of their activity in terms of the group's efforts; in other words, their efforts have an impact if the group has an impact. A second strategy is to reduce the cognitive dissonance created by the perceived discrepancy between the amount of effort they make and the potential impact of their contribution by "credit claiming"—that is, by taking disproportionate credit for the effects of the group's activities or by ignoring the relative size of their contribution to the group's activities. A third strategy is to emphasize the outcomes of interactions within the group rather than the effects of group activities.[30]

A recent formulation of a rational-actor theory of voting, which also focuses on the role of entrepreneurs, suggests that group leaders, through manipulation of the stimuli presented to individuals, can enhance citizens' normative sense of group identity and their awareness of the importance of a particular political outcome to group members. Group leaders bargain with politicians to augment group benefits. The closer the politicians' issue positions are to those preferred by group members, the greater will be the group members' support for those politicians through political participation. The implications are that individuals participate in collective action in part because of their normative commitments to the group, and that collective action is stimulated by group leaders through effective bargaining with political leaders. The individual group members gain through both policy benefits (which may be small) and "consumption" (participation) benefits. This model has been summarized as follows:

Group elites provide their members or identifiers with incentives to vote in order to capture a collective benefit for the group through shifts in candidate position. Leaders jockey for position in turnout space as candidates move in policy space; the leaders' payoffs consist of policies, while the candidates' payoffs consist of votes. The individual voters' payoffs consist of a small policy term and a large consumption benefit.[31]

This formulation rests upon a distinction between an *interest group*—a group that is organized to make demands on government—and a *reference group,* a group with which an individual identifies and whose perceived norms guide the individual's behavior. Leaders stimulate reference-group identification, and when the reference group becomes an interest group, leaders endorse those politicians who support the group's demands and direct communications at group members urging their support.

Underlying this thesis is the view that group leaders rely on psychological as well as material incentives. The sense of reference-group membership and individuals' commitment to the group play significant roles in motivating members to engage in collective action. The commitment is group-specific and subject to manipulation by group leaders to increase expenditure of individual resources (such as time, money, effort, talent, and votes) to obtain benefits for the reference group (votes in Congress against an immigration bill or in support of an import quota, or a commitment from the president or a legislator to support a constitutional amendment authorizing school prayer). Research has demonstrated that reference-group identification does have a significant impact on voter turnout.[32]

Another solution to the problem of organizational formation has been formulated in terms of "contract by coordination," which means mutual agreement on a strategy that satisfactorily rewards all participants in the activity. This mutual agreement can occur in two ways: All participants may realize, through reasoning processes, that a particular strategy is the best for each to pursue, or participants may go through a set of reward-and-punishment experiences from which they learn which is the strategy that maximizes their utility.[33]

The question of whether to contribute to the attainment of a collective good can be considered as a problem in strategic decision making in which individuals must analyze the effects of the alternative choices that they could make when the outcome depends both on their choice and on the choices that others make. One method of assessing the effects is game theory, which was developed in the late 1930s and early 1940s by mathematicians and has been elaborated since then by social scientists for the analysis of strategic decision-making problems.[34] Imagine two men arrested by the police and charged with a serious crime. If either is incriminated by the other, he faces a ten-year sentence; if neither incriminates the other, the police will then have less evidence but the two can be convicted on a less serious charge, leading to a sentence of only three years. The prosecutor has promised each prisoner a one-year reduction of either sentence if he does testify against the other. The various sentencing possibilities are shown in the following table (a "payoff matrix"), where the first number in each pair represents the sentence for prisoner A and the second number the sentence for prisoner B:

| | | Prisoner A | |
		Be silent	Testify
Prisoner B	Be silent	3, 3	2, 10
	Testify	10, 2	9, 9

Thus, each is best off if he testifies against the other while the other remains silent, but each is worse off if he remains silent while the other testifies against him. If both remain silent or both testify, the outcomes are indeterminate. Since the police do not allow the two to talk to each other, neither knows what the other is going to do, and so it is intrinsically difficult for them to know which decision on their part would be in their own best interest. This kind of situation has been called the "prisoner's dilemma."

As another example of such a situation, suppose the people in a neighborhood want to build a swimming pool for their use, and they form an association for that purpose. The pool will cost $100,000, so if all 500 households join, the cost will be $200 each. If only half of them join, the cost will be $400 to each of them—but for the other half, the pool will be free. If only one-quarter of them join, the cost would be $800 each—and facing that kind of cost, they may decide not to join and the pool will not be built. Should a family join, on the assumption that others will join and share the cost, or should it not join, let others bear the cost, and run the risk of not having the pool at all?

To take a real-life example on a larger scale, consider the case of Chesapeake Bay. The bay is home to many varieties of fish, shellfish, and waterfowl. Pollution of the bay's waters by inadequately treated waste from city and county sewage-treatment plants is destroying the animal and plant life on which the fish and fowl depend. Should a city spend money to build a new treatment plant? If only one city does, the pollution will not be reduced very much, and the voters in that city might feel that their money had been wasted. If all the cities that contribute to the pollution build new treatment plants, they will all benefit from the improved conditions in the bay—but none of them can be sure that all the others will do so. Faced with such a situation, environmentalists might form or join organizations such as the Sierra Club or the Chesapeake Bay Foundation to lobby for government programs that would induce or force local governments—and perhaps also corporations, farmers, and others—to take measures to reduce the pollution.

Collective-action problems can be treated as an iterated prisoner's-dilemma game in which "coordination by convention" develops. (*Iterated* means that the same players make similar kinds of strategic choices over and over again, as for example when members of Congress vote on several energy-policy issues during the course of a number of congressional sessions.) A convention to cooperate in obtaining the collective good develops only if there are incentives to cooperate, the participants know each others' preferences and perceptions of the situation, and the same situations are repeated.[35] Hardin argues that the overlapping nature of much group activity increases the possibility that coordination by convention will occur and also facilitates the enforcement of such conventions. Conventions are honored because participants in the interaction learn that it is in their interest to adhere to them.[36]

Axelrod, on the other hand, presents a case for coordination in collective-action situations through reward-and-punishment processes. Using computer-simulation methods and testing a number of solutions to a prisoner's-dilemma game against each other, Axelrod found that the best decision rule, dubbed "TIT FOR TAT," followed a reward-and-punishment strategy that enabled the player pursuing it to attain as favorable an outcome as he could expect by following any other strategy. The TIT-FOR-TAT strategy is to cooperate on the first play, then respond to the other player's previous move on each subsequent play. While a participant pursuing this strategy does not do substantially better than other players, he does not do any worse.[37] Axelrod describes the TIT-FOR-TAT strategy as being nice, forgiving, retaliatory, and clear.

Piotr Swistak argues that strategies that are fair and unexploitable are superior for tournaments of iterated games, with TIT FOR TAT being appropriate for certain kinds of environments. Those environments are tournaments of iterated games with two kinds of players—natives and invaders—in which sophisticated players determine their strategies before the tournament, do not change during the course of the tournament, do not know the strategies their opponents will use, and seek to maximize their scores over the entire tournament rather than to win any one play. Swistak demonstrates that a set of strategies that have the characteristics of being fair and unexploitable is superior, with TIT FOR TAT being more limited. Such strategies provide for greater flexibility than TIT FOR TAT, in that a player may choose to defect at any time and restore cooperation at any time. Swistak provides a proof for the theorem that

If TIT FOR TAT plays in a tournament with fair and unexploitable strategies, and if the length of the tournament is such that every player has a chance to retaliate against its opponent's defection, then TIT FOR TAT wins the tournament.[38]

For asymmetric games with more than two kinds of populations, Swistak argues that the best strategies are nice, unexploitable, and envious.[39]

Cooperation could be promoted by increasing the costs of noncooperation ("enlarging the shadow of the future"), making the payoffs for cooperation greater, and teaching participants the values, facts, and skills that underlie cooperation.[40] This assumes that participation in collective action activities from a self-interested basis is learned behavior. An alternative view is that cooperative behavior is innate, and that it is egoistic, narrowly self-interested behavior that is learned.[41]

While the usual choice in prisoner's-dilemma games is only between cooperation and defection, a third choice is possible: exit, or refusing to play the game altogether. Certainly that option exists in various types of real-world situations; for example, people who don't like the policies of a city, county, or state may leave it and move elsewhere.[42] One set of experimental studies reports that where this option is provided, exit rates are lower in groups where discussion is permitted, and higher among participants whose initial choice was noncooperation than among those who at first cooperated.[43] The role of a sense of justice or fairness in determining collective-action strategies has also been demonstrated in the experimental studies.[44]

A quite different solution to the problem of explaining why individuals contribute to collective action has been labeled the "fair share" model by its developer, Howard Margolis. This model also assumes rationality, but defines it as "consistency of choice" in individual behavior.[45] It is further assumed that individuals see utility both in pursuing their self-interest and in contributing to the welfare of others. The latter is based on two kinds of motivation—"goods altruism" and "participation altruism." Goods altruism means that the individual "gains utility from an increase in the goods available to others: his utility function incorporates a taste for having other people better off."[46] The utility of participation altruism is the utility gained from the act of giving resources away for the benefit of others.

The concepts of participation altruism and goods altruism are important in the fair-share model in accounting for the individual's distribution of resources between self-interest and group interest. An individual varies the weight given to self-interest; the one who has given less to the group in the past is motivated to give more in the future, up to the point where an equilibrium between self-interest and group interest occurs. The equilibrium point will vary with the individual's valuation of group interest, the individual's needs at a given point in time, and the resources available to the individual.[47] Margolis describes the decision to allocate resources between oneself and the group in the following way:

The larger the share of my resources I have spent unselfishly, the more weight I give to my selfish interests in allocating marginal resources. On the other hand, the larger the benefit I can confer on the group compared with the benefit from spending marginal resources on myself, the more I will tend to act unselfishly.[48]

Spending on the group interest under this allocation rule is a superior good, and those who have higher incomes allocate a greater share of their resources to group interests.

Group interest can be of several types. One is based on kinship or family. Another is reciprocal, such as that growing out of the patterns of cooperative interaction. A third is "group-focused altruism," in which individuals are not motivated by any sort of benefit to themselves. Group-focused altruism can be strengthened by increasing the importance of future considerations in current decision making, increasing the payoffs to those who allocate resources to the group, and deliberately inculcating values, skills, and facts that promote cooperative behavior.[49] Because for most individuals the resources allocated to group interest are quite small compared to the resources allocated to self-interest, most decisions about both the quantity of resources to allocate to group interest and their distribution among various instruments of group interest are probably based on a minimal information search. To develop decisions on the basis of full information would be an inefficient use of the resources that are allocated to group interest.[50] Representing the ordinary citizen as *Smith,* and the resources devoted to group interests as *G,* Margolis observes:

In a large society, both Smith's spending and the benefits from that spending will be microscopically small from a social point of view. It will often be hard, therefore, for Smith to "see" the ratio of benefit to cost directly in terms of his own act. However, it may be quite easy to estimate this ratio (in particular to compare this ratio across alternative ways of using G resources) in terms of a judgment about the ratio of aggregate benefits and costs of everyone in Smith's position behaving in a certain way.[51]

In Margolis's view, G resources are not considered to benefit personally the individual providing the resources.

In another critique of the view that individuals are rational egoists, economist A. K. Sen argues that individuals' choices may be influenced by sympathy (concern for others that directly affects one's own sense of welfare and is therefore egoistic) or by commitment (concern about situations that directly affect others but do not make the individual feel personally worse off). Sen's concept of commitment is similar to Margolis's group altruism, in that it assumes that individuals may choose outcomes that would not serve their own narrowly defined self-interest.[52]

The economic model of collective action assumes that individual preferences that reflect human needs are fixed. Logically, however, collective-choice decisions could vary with shifts in individual preference orderings. Such a notion is not unknown in either philosophy or economics,[53] but it greatly complicates both the theorizing and the research that use a political-economy approach to the analysis of political decisions. Frankfurt argues that individuals can simultaneously hold several different preference orderings, using different ones as the basis for decision making at different times. He sees individuals as having not only first-order desires, which are ascertainable from the choices they make (a standard assumption in rational choice theory), but also second-order desires, which may not coincide with their first-order preferences. Individual choices frequently involve determining which set of preference orderings should be operational in a particular situation.

Another explanation of the formation and maintenance of groups that pursue collective goods without reliance on selective incentives requires a reconsideration of what is classified as costs or benefits. It has already been noted that some individuals derive enjoyment from—in effect, benefit from—the act of participating in politics. These "political junkies" work to form groups and to obtain group goals in part for the enjoyment gained from the activity. The enjoyment may be either socially or purposively (goal-attainment) oriented.[54] Several studies of participation in political-party activity report the importance of both these types of incentives.[55]

Hirschman is another who argues that in the pursuit of public action, both the actions aimed at obtaining the desired collective good and the collective good itself have positive value. In other words, what rational-choice theory considers to be costs are in many instances, to the citizens who are engaging in collective action, part of the benefit.[56] Perhaps, however, this does not apply equally to the pursuit of all collective goods, but primarily to the pursuit of those that affect the quality of life for the individuals themselves and for others, as they perceive the situation. Thus, the quality of the Chesapeake Bay is, to many of those concerned with it, not an economic matter; to those who earn their living from fishing in the bay, however, it is very much an economic concern. Similarly, most people active in groups seeking action to combat acid rain do not depend on forestry in the Appalachian Mountains, New England, or Canada for their living; rather, they are concerned that the general quality of life for themselves and for future citizens will be diminished by the degradation of the lakes, streams, and forests of the affected areas.

Efforts to expand the theory of collective action in the ways that have been discussed here have met with a number of objections. One is that they alter the nature of the problem being studied, changing the focus to the behavior of individuals rather than the behavior of groups. But this is specious reasoning, for individual motivations in making contributions to group action underlie collective-action theory and the analysis of the formation and the maintenance of groups. A second objection is that adding variables to the theory does not increase its explanatory power, for the behavior of individuals in group settings can be adequately explained with the use of individual calculations of costs and benefits, narrowly defined.[57]

Several different solutions to the "Olson problem" suggested by scholars have been considered. The role of entrepreneurs in the establishment and maintenance of organizations seeking collective goods has been examined in three studies based on samples of national organizations or of their members.[58] A number of experimental studies have examined the incidence and in some cases the evolution of cooperation by convention, but field research has been limited to a few analyses of coalition formation in the national policy arena. The degree to which generalization is possible on the basis of computer simulations and laboratory experiments can be questioned,[59] but the evidence from many of these studies does suggest that purely egoistic behavior occurs less frequently than Olson's theory implies.

Summary

Is participation rational? Obviously, the answer to that question depends on how the term *rational* is defined. If rationality is taken to mean consistency in choices, then it is easy to observe in patterns of political participation. If to be rational means to be a utility maximizer, and utility is narrowly defined as immediate personal benefit exceeding the cost of participating, then many types of political participation are not rational.

Is voting rational? If it is to be considered rational only if any one individual's vote makes a significant difference in the outcome of an election, then voting usually is not rational. However, other impacts may be taken into account by citizens in evaluating the utility of voting. These include the psychic rewards obtained from the act of participating, from conforming to a social norm that calls for participation, and from the sense of contributing to the survival of the political system (the long-run participation value). Individuals can also derive satisfaction from joining with others to vote for or against candidates on the basis of a particular issue about which the members of the group feel very strongly and on the outcome of which they believe that their vote shares an effect.

While scholars do not agree on how to account for the formation and maintenance of groups that pursue collective goods, it is obvious that such groups do form. Those that do are probably a biased sample of all possible groups that might be created to seek a collective good. Debate continues as to the types of incentives that motivate individuals to contribute to the provision of a collective good either through the activities of a group's members or through their efforts to have the government distribute the cost of the collective good's provision to all members of society.

NOTES

1. Anthony Downs, *An Economic Theory of Democracy* (New York: Harper and Row, 1957), 5.
2. Russell Hardin, *Collective Action* (Baltimore: Johns Hopkins University Press, 1982), 10.
3. Terry M. Moe, *The Organization of Interests* (Chicago: University of Chicago Press, 1980), 3.
4. William H. Riker and Peter C. Ordeshook, *An Introduction to Positive Political Theory* (Englewood Cliffs, N.J.: Prentice Hall, 1973), 20.
5. Norman Frohlich, Joe A. Oppenheimer, and Oran Young, *Political Leadership and Collective Goods* (Princeton: Princeton University Press, 1971), 26–29.
6. Moe, *Organization of Interests*, 14.
7. Riker and Ordeshook, *Positive Political Theory*, 63.
8. Downs, *Economic Theory of Democracy*, 266–271.
9. Ibid., 260–261.
10. Riker and Ordeshook, *Positive Political Theory*, 62–63.
11. Paul Meehl, "The Selfish Voter Paradox and the Thrown Away Vote Argument," *American Political Science Review* 71 (1977): 11–30.
12. John Ferejohn and Morris Fiorina, "The Paradox of Not Voting," *American Political Science Review* 68 (1974): 525–536.
13. Robert Goodin and K.W.S. Roberts, "The Ethical Voter," *American Political Science Review* 69 (1975): 925–928.
14. Carole Jean Uhlaner, "Political Participation, Rational Actors, and Rationality: A New Approach," *Political Psychology* 7 (1986): 551–557.
15. Carole J. Uhlaner, "Rational Turnout: The Neglected Role of Groups," *American Journal of Political Science* 33 (1989): 390–422; Carole J. Uhlaner, " 'Relational Goods' and Participation: Incorporating Sociability into a Theory of Rational Action," *Public Choice* 62(3) (1988): 253–285.
16. John F. Zipp, "Perceived Representativeness and Voting: An Assessment of the Impact of 'Choices' vs. 'Echoes'," *American Political Science Review* 79 (1985): 50–61.
17. Gregory Brunk, "The Impact of Rational Participation Models on Voting Attitudes," *Public Choice* 35 (1980): 549–564.
18. American National Election Studies (1976), Center for Political Studies, University of Michigan.
19. For discussions of the nature of collective goods, see Mancur Olson, *The Logic of Collective Action* (Cambridge: Harvard University Press, 1971), 14–16; and Hardin, *Collective Action*, 16–20.
20. Olson, *Logic of Collective Action*, 2.
21. Ibid., 20–36.
22. Assuming a fixed number of participants N and the cost of the total good C which has a value V to individual i, the subset k that would be large enough to benefit from providing the good would be "the smallest integer larger than C/V." Hardin, *Collective Action*, 42–49.
23. See, for example, Gerald Marvell and Ruth E. Ames, "Experiments on the Provision of Public Goods: I. Resources, Interest, Group Size, and the Free Rider Problem," *American Journal of Sociology* 84 (1979): 1335–1360; Gerald Marvell and Ruth E. Ames, "Experiments on the Provision of Public Goods: II. Provision Points, Experiences, and the Free Rider Problem," *American Journal of Sociology* 85 (1980): 927–937; and Norman Frohlich and Joe A. Oppenheimer, "Beyond Economic Man: Altruism, Egalitarianism, and Difference Maximizing," *Journal of Conflict Resolution* 28 (1984): 3–24. Results of survey research examining the effect of public goods, altruistic motives, and social as well as private incentives in stimulating participation in collective action are presented in Edward N. Muller and Karl-Dieter Opp, "Rational Choice and Rebellious Collective Action: Public Goods, Psychological Gratification, and

Socialist Class Consciousness" (paper delivered at the annual meeting of the American Political Science Association, Washington, D.C., August 30–September 2, 1984); and Karl-Dieter Opp, "Soft Incentives and Collective Action," unpublished paper, Department of Sociology, University of Hamburg, November 1983.

24. See Jack Walker, "The Origins and Maintenance of Interest Groups in America," *American Political Science Review* 77 (1983): 983, figure 1. The increase in the number of groups appears to have been stimulated by outside resources as well as by member resources.

25. Jeffrey M. Berry, *The Interest Group Society* (Boston: Little, Brown, 1984); Jeffrey M. Berry, *Lobbying for the People* (Princeton: Princeton University Press, 1977); M. Margaret Conway, "PACs, the New Politics, and Congressional Campaigns," in *Interest Group Politics*, ed. A. Cigler and B. Loomis (Washington, D.C.: CQ Press, 1983), 126–144; and Robert C. Mitchell, "National Environmental Lobbies and the Apparent Illogic of Collective Action," in *Collective Decision Making*, ed. Clifford S. Russell (Baltimore: Johns Hopkins University Press, 1979), 87–121.

26. Norman Frohlich and Joe A. Oppenheimer, "I Get By with a Little Help from My Friends," *World Politics* 23 (1970): 104–120; Moe, *Organization of Interests*, 37–39; Frohlich, Oppenheimer, and Young, *Political Leadership*; Robert H. Salisbury, "An Exchange Theory of Interest Groups," *Midwest Journal of Political Science* 13 (1969): 1–32; and Richard Wagner, "Pressure Groups and Political Entrepreneurs: A Review Article," in *Papers on Non-Market Decision Making*, ed. Gordon Tullock (Charlottesville: University of Virginia Press, 1966), 161–170.

27. Moe, *Organization of Interests*, chap. 3.

28. Ibid., 57.

29. Uhlaner, "Rational Turnout"; Uhlaner, "'Relational Goods' and Participation"; Moe, *Organization of Interests*, 114; Brian Barry, *Sociologists, Economists, and Democracy* (Chicago: University of Chicago Press, 1977), 33.

30. Karl-Dieter Opp, "Economics, Sociology, and Political Protest," in *Theoretical Models and Empirical Analyses: Contributions to the Explanation of Individual Actions and Collective Phenomena*, ed. W. Raub (Groningen, Netherlands: Utrecht, 1982), 166–185.

31. Uhlaner, "Political Participation, Rational Actors, and Rationality."

32. Arthur H. Miller, Patricia Gurin, Gerald Gurin, and Oksana Malanchuk, "Group Consciousness and Political Participation," *American Journal of Political Science* 25 (1981): 495–511; and M. Margaret Conway, "Group Identification, Perceived Group Interest, and Patterns of Political Participation" (paper delivered at the annual meeting of the Western Political Science Association, Denver, March 26–28, 1981).

33. Hardin, *Collective Action*, 155–156 and chap. 10; and Robert Axelrod, *The Evolution of Cooperation* (New York: Basic Books, 1984), 12–19.

34. Game theory was originally developed largely by John von Neumann and Oskar Morgenstern; see their *Theory of Games and Economic Behavior* (Princeton: Princeton University Press, 1944). Anatol Rapoport played a major role in the evolution of its use in psychology and other social sciences; see his *Two-Person Game Theory* (Ann Arbor: University of Michigan Press, 1966) and *N-Person Game Theory* (Ann Arbor: University of Michigan Press, 1970). Another early exposition of the ideas underlying the social-science applications of game theory is R. Duncan Luce and Howard Raiffa, *Games and Decisions* (New York: John Wiley & Sons, 1957).

35. Hardin, *Collective Action*, 172.

36. Ibid., 175. See also Robert Axelrod, *The Evolution of Cooperation* (New York: Basic Books, 1984), chap. 6; David Lewis, *Convention* (Cambridge: Harvard University Press, 1982).

37. Axelrod, *Evolution of Cooperation*, 31–32.

38. Piotr Swistak, "A Theory of Tournaments of Iterated Prisoner's Dilemma Game" (working paper, Department of Government and Politics, University of Maryland, College Park, November 1989); Piotr Swistak, "Stability and Invasion in Tournaments of Iterated Prisoner's Dilemma Game" (working paper, Department of Government and Politics, University of Maryland, College Park, January 1990).

39. Piotr Swistak, personal communication, March 12, 1990.

40. Axelrod, *Evolution of Cooperation,* chap. 7.

41. Uhlaner, "Political Participation," 566–567. See also Carol Gilligan, *In a Different Voice* (Cambridge: Harvard University Press, 1982).

42. Albert O. Hirschman, *Exit, Voice, and Loyalty* (Cambridge: Harvard University Press, 1970).

43. John Orbell, Peregine Schwartz-Shea, and Randy T. Simmons, "Do Cooperators Exit More Readily than Defectors?" *American Political Science Review* 78 (1984): 147–162.

44. Frohlich and Oppenheimer, "Beyond Economic Man," 9–16.

45. Howard Margolis, *Selfishness, Altruism, and Rationality* (Cambridge: Cambridge University Press, 1984), 6, 14.

46. Ibid., 21.

47. Ibid., 29.

48. Ibid., 36.

49. Axelrod, *Evolution of Cooperation,* chap. 7.

50. Margolis, *Selfishness,* 49–50.

51. Ibid., 51.

52. Amartya K. Sen, "Rational Fools: A Critique of the Behavioral Foundations of Economic Theory," *Philosophy and Public Affairs* 6 (1977): 326–329.

53. Harry G. Frankfurt, "Freedom of the Will and the Concept of a Person," *Journal of Philosophy* 58 (1971): 5–20; and Sen, "Rational Fools."

54. James Q. Wilson, *Political Organizations* (New York: Basic Books, 1973).

55. Samuel Eldersveld, *Political Parties: A Behavioral Analysis* (Chicago: Rand McNally, 1964); M. Margaret Conway and Frank B. Feigert, "Motivation, Incentive Systems, and the Political Party Organization," *American Political Science Review* 62 (1978): 1159–1173; and Peter Gluck, "Research Note: Incentives and the Maintenance of Political Styles in Different Locales," *Western Political Quarterly* 25 (1972): 753–760.

56. Albert O. Hirschman, *Shifting Involvements* (Princeton: Princeton University Press, 1982), 85–86 and 126.

57. Hardin, *Collective Action,* 14.

58. Barry, *Sociologists;* Mitchell, "National Environmental Lobbies"; and Thomas L. Gais, Mark A. Peterson, and Jack L. Walker, "Interest Groups, Iron Triangles, and Representative Institutions in American National Government," *British Journal of Political Science* (1984): 161–185.

59. When an experiment defines the choice as being between personal and group interest, social pressure may produce a biased distribution of results. (See, for example, Hardin, *Collective Action,* 114). Although research designs attempt to control these factors, that may not always be possible. Thus, experimental designs may not capture reality sufficiently well to permit valid generalizations to real-world choice situations. See also Robert E. Goodin, "Itinerants, Iterations, and Something In-Between," *British Journal of Political Science* 14 (1984): 129–132.

Chapter 7

Explanations of Patterns
of Participation

The discussion in the preceding chapters has examined several different types of factors that contribute to an understanding of who participates in politics and in what ways and to what extent they do so. The life circumstances of citizens, their psychological orientations to politics, the political and legal environment in which they exist, the laws and governmental rules that regulate participation, and the choices citizens make about their participation—all these influence the patterns of participation. The question addressed in this chapter is the weight of these factors relative to each other.

Unfortunately, only a partial answer to that question can be provided because the data necessary for a complete answer are not available. Survey results containing a full set of good measures for all five types of relevant explanatory factors do not exist, and measures of some kinds of participation are not included in all the data sets that do exist. Lastly, the same measures of important explanatory variables have not been used in different studies.[1]

As already noted, voting turnout has been studied in surveys of the electorate in every national election since 1952. Since some people claim that they have voted when they did not, "voter validation" studies have been conducted, checking respondents' reported voting participation against the actual voting participation recorded in the files of the registration or election board in those jurisdictions where such records are kept.[2] However, these records are not available in all jurisdictions and voter-validation studies have not been conducted for all election surveys. Nevertheless, some valid generalizations can be drawn from self-reports of voting turnout.[3]

Measures of other forms of participation have less frequently been included in the national surveys, but analysis of the relative influence upon them of various types of explanatory factors is possible to some degree.

Trends in Voter Turnout

Voting participation in presidential elections declined substantially from 1960 to 1988 outside the South. (In the eleven southern states, voter turnout increased slightly after 1964 as a consequence of the removal of legal and administrative barriers to political participation and the changing economic and social climate in the South; see Chapter 5.) Tables 7-1 and 7-2 present some of the patterns of voter turnout in the nonsouthern states during those years.

If individuals are to respond to their political environment, they must become aware of it. Television has become an increasingly common source of political information, yet a television news program can present only a very limited amount of information. The script for a half-hour program could be printed on one-half of one page of a newspaper. Meanwhile, the proportion of the electorate that reports regularly reading stories about the campaign in a newspaper has declined from almost half in 1960 to approximately one-quarter in 1980. As Table 7-1 indicates, less frequent users of the print-news media are less likely to vote than are more frequent print-news media consumers.

While the psychological-involvement variables show strong effects, these effects are altered by changes in the proportion of citizens at different levels of the variables. For example, although voters high in political efficacy have regularly been 20 to 30 percent more likely to vote than those low in political efficacy, a smaller proportion of the electorate had high levels of political efficacy in the 1970s and 1980s (see Chapter 3). The effect of party identification is complicated by a change in its relationship to turnout. The proportion of the electorate that calls itself "in-

TABLE 7-1

Reported Voter Turnout Outside the South in Presidential Elections, 1960–1988, by Selected Psychological Variables

Variable	Category	1960	1964	1968	1972	1976	1980	1984	1988
Political efficacy	High	90.5	85.8	87.0	85.7	85.9	85.2	—	—
	Medium	77.7	79.2	79.9	73.5	74.2	74.0	—	—
	Low	60.0	76.9	63.3	64.5	64.1	56.8	—	—
Party identification	Strong Democratic	82.6	85.2	85.9	79.6	82.7	85.2	91.9	72.6
	Weak Democratic	81.0	79.3	73.3	73.0	70.1	67.0	68.9	63.9
	Independent Democratic	74.0	77.3	72.6	74.4	77.1	69.0	70.7	61.6
	Independent	83.3	64.0	64.4	56.5	63.1	53.9	64.3	49.3
	Independent Republican	88.5	86.2	83.5	81.6	77.1	78.4	75.1	59.7
	Weak Republican	89.8	86.8	83.9	80.3	75.7	77.3	78.3	70.0
	Strong Republican	92.4	94.1	87.1	89.7	93.1	89.6	89.2	83.9
Political trust[a]	High	—	85.4	78.3	82.1	79.8	68.4	81.8	—
	Medium high	—	82.5	79.7	79.6	76.0	80.3	77.4	82.7
	Medium	—	81.5	84.1	82.6	77.9	74.4	77.5	78.5
	Medium low	—	82.7	82.8	74.5	73.9	71.4	78.4	70.3
	Low	—	78.9	68.6	66.2	75.8	74.0	75.1	47.1
Frequency of reading newspaper articles on the campaign	Regularly	90.5	89.8	88.7	90.6	88.9	—	96.3	80.8
	Often	89.3	87.4	87.6	83.3	88.0	90.2[b]	91.4	84.2
	From time to time	87.3	83.5	80.9	76.5	77.4	79.0[b]	81.2	79.5
	Once in a great while	80.2	71.7	73.5	51.7	66.5	65.6[b]	72.9	67.2
	None	63.0	66.8	55.0	67.8	52.5	50.0[b]	62.1	50.0

SOURCES: Data for 1960–1976 from Stephen D. Shaffer, "A Multivariate Explanation of Decreasing Turnout in Presidential Elections, 1960–1976," *American Journal of Political Science* 25 (1981): 76–77, table 3. Copyright © 1981 University of Texas Press. Reprinted by permission. Data for 1980, 1984, and 1988 from the American National Election Studies, Center for Political Studies, University of Michigan.

[a] This index is based on four items, one of which is differently worded from 1974 to 1984.

[b] In 1980 the question was phrased somewhat differently. In answer to, "How many newspaper articles did you read about the campaign?" the choice of answers was "a good many," "several," "just one or two," and "none."

TABLE 7-2

Reported Voter Turnout Outside the South in Presidential Elections, 1960–1988, by Age and Education

	1960	1964	1968	1972	1976	1980	1984	1988
Age								
21–24	55.6	61.3	58.8	69.5	62.2	51.0	56.9	43.3
25–28	74.8	69.9	67.0	78.2	66.7	58.3	61.3	48.0
29–32	77.5	82.5	75.7	81.5	65.7	68.1	76.4	56.1
33–36	90.4	78.9	82.1	72.9	75.9	70.0	82.6	65.8
37–40	80.3	86.0	78.4	78.2	83.3	79.5	82.5	73.6
41–44	87.7	89.8	81.4	81.0	84.7	78.3	80.9	77.7
45–48	94.8	86.0	89.8	86.3	84.3	80.0	78.8	76.9
49–52	92.6	83.3	81.0	82.8	79.8	76.5	83.1	70.0
53–56	75.5	92.9	88.2	60.3	81.3	82.0	85.7	76.8
57–60	89.7	88.9	75.4	78.0	83.7	81.7	91.5	68.0
61–64	92.4	87.5	84.8	73.2	80.0	82.4	83.5	81.4
65–68	90.2	88.9	85.4	78.6	77.4	93.0	86.2	73.3
69–72	95.9	83.3	76.5	74.2	82.1	84.4	89.8	83.1
73–76	80.0	89.3	75.8	66.7	84.9	80.6	81.3	80.0
77 +	56.8	75.0	67.6	66.7	56.5	60.0	69.4	62.0
Years of education								
0–8	75.8	74.5	63.0	59.6	65.3	57.9	60.6	51.6
9–11	77.2	77.5	69.9	65.7	59.7	53.6	60.2	50.3
12	89.4	84.7	85.3	80.7	72.8	71.5	72.3	62.8
Some college	90.8	89.6	85.6	87.5	87.5	83.2	86.4	81.7

SOURCES: Data for 1960–1976 from Stephen D. Shaffer, "A Multivariate Explanation of Decreasing Turnout in Presidential Elections, 1960–1976," *American Journal of Political Science* 25 (1981): 76–77, table 3. Copyright © 1981 University of Texas Press. Reprinted by permission. Data for 1980, 1984, and 1988 from the American National Election Studies, Center for Political Studies, University of Michigan.

dependent" has increased, at the expense of the proportion identifying with one party or the other; but, as Table 7-1 shows, independents are generally less likely to vote than identifiers, and the decline in turnout has been even greater among independents than among identifiers. There has also been a consistent pattern across the years of both strong and weak identifiers with the Democratic party being less likely to vote than strong and weak identifiers with the Republican party.

Among educational categories (Table 7-2), the decline in turnout has been most severe (27 percent) among those with nine to eleven years of educational attainment, and nearly as large among those with a high-school diploma, compared to a decline of less than 9 percent among the college educated. However, the effect of those differences is moderated by the fact that the educational level of the electorate has been rising, so that there are fewer people in the low-education categories.

Similar patterns of relationship exist in the midterm congressional elections (Tables 7-3 and 7-4). For example, Democrats (except in 1986) are generally less likely to vote than Republicans, and those who are independents are less likely to vote than are identifiers with either party. However, independents who perceived themselves as closer to one of the major parties (labeled "leaners" in Table 7-3) were less likely to vote than were weak party identifiers in 1970, 1982, and 1986, but more likely to vote in 1974 and 1978. In 1986, Democratic leaners were slightly less likely to vote than were Democratic weak identifiers, but Republican leaners were more likely to vote than that party's weak identifiers.

Those who cared more about the outcome of the election were much more likely to vote in midterm elections than were those who cared less. (This variable was not included in the studies of presidential elections.) The relationships between voting turnout and age and education are the same in midterm elections as in presidential elections.

Accounting for Turnout

A number of scholars have attempted to assess the relative impact of the various factors that might account for the patterns of voter turnout, and especially for its decline. Some have focused on a limited set of variables,[4] while others have attempted to be more inclusive.[5] The research designs and the methods of analysis used have varied significantly. Where similar conclusions are drawn from studies of different elections using different models and methods, the inferences drawn have greater reliability.

The evidence is quite strong that two aspects of psychological involvement in politics—political efficacy and partisan identification—have played a significant role in the decline in voting participation since 1960. One set of analyses concludes that ap-

TABLE 7-3

Reported Voter Turnout in Midterm Congressional Elections, *1970–1986, by Selected Psychological Variables*

Variable and category	1970	1974	1978	1982	1986
Party identification					
Strong Democrat	51.8	57.8	54.9	75.9	67.1
Weak Democrat	41.0	42.3	36.2	59.5	50.9
Independent					
Democrat	36.7	46.7	40.7	51.6	49.6
Independent	29.0	26.2	27.2	35.5	31.2
Independent					
Republican	41.6	49.0	53.3	62.5	55.1
Weak Republican	54.2	53.8	51.2	59.9	50.2
Strong Republican	66.4	70.1	65.3	80.0	67.8
lambda	.11	.15	.11	.04	.05
Strength of party identification					
Independent	29.0	26.2	27.2	35.5	31.2
Leaners	38.8	47.6	45.7	56.2	52.4
Weak party identifiers	45.9	46.9	41.4	59.6	50.6
Strong party identifiers	55.9	61.7	58.5	77.2	67.4
tau	.19[a]	.22[a]	.17[a]	.22[a]	.29[a]
Political efficacy					
Low	32.5	35.7	37.5	—	—
1	40.5	43.0	38.0	—	—
2	47.2	49.2	41.4	—	—
3	53.4	63.9	50.0	—	—
4	59.5	66.9	61.2	—	—
tau	.20[a]	.20[a]	.14[a]		
Care about outcome of elections					
Low	7.8	16.0	18.7	27.8	17.7
2	26.4	29.6	37.6	46.1	38.4
3	54.4	56.9	54.9	70.2	66.3
High	66.1	72.8	64.8	84.1	79.2
tau	.40[a]	.45[a]	.33[a]	.35[a]	.60[a]

SOURCES: M. Margaret Conway, "Political Participation in Midterm Congressional Elections: Attitudinal and Social Characteristics during the 1970s," *American Politics Quarterly* 9 (1981): 221–244. Copyright © 1981; reprinted by permission of Sage Publications, Inc. And the 1982 and 1986 American National Election Studies, Center for Political Studies, University of Michigan.

Note: All numbers, except lambda and tau, are percentages.

[a]p = .001.

TABLE 7-4

Reported Voter Turnout in Midterm Congressional Elections,
1970–1986, by Age, Income, and Education

Variable and category	1970	1974	1978	1982	1986
Age					
18–29	27.0	28.1	23.7	36.5	30.1
30–39	42.7	45.3	42.1	63.8	47.2
40–49	53.4	53.8	50.0	69.7	59.8
50–59	57.9	55.5	55.6	72.0	68.7
60–65	53.1	72.6	59.6	71.0	70.7
Over 65	49.5	53.4	54.6	65.8	69.4
tau	.21[a]	.27[a]	.28[a]	.19[a]	.42[a]
Income percentile					
0–16	42.5	38.7	45.7	45.6	37.6
17–33	54.2	49.1	46.4	54.2	46.3
34–67	56.0	49.9	56.2	65.7	52.7
68–95	71.5	64.6	60.7	67.8	62.8
96–100	77.8	75.0	72.6	67.7	65.1
Years of education					
8 years or less	37.2	38.6	38.1	44.8	45.4
9–11 years	33.1	35.7	28.0	40.8	32.3
Completed high school	46.0	44.7	41.3	59.1	50.2
1–3 years of college	50.7	51.5	46.4	66.6	59.6
4 years of college	76.4	65.7	52.9	74.7	71.0
Advanced degree	73.8	73.4	67.9	79.8	74.1
tau	.22[a]	.21[a]	.19[a]	.20[a]	.34[a]

SOURCES: M. Margaret Conway, "Political Participation in Midterm Congressional Elections: Attitudinal and Social Characteristics during the 1970s," *American Politics Quarterly* 9 (1981): 221–244. Copyright © 1981; reprinted by permission of Sage Publications, Inc. And the 1982 and 1986 American National Election Studies, Center for Political Studies, University of Michigan. For income percentile figures, Warren E. Miller and Santa A. Traugott, *American National Election Studies Data Sourcebook 1952–1986* (Cambridge: Harvard University Press, 1989), 305, table 5.23.

Note: All numbers, except tau, are percentages.
[a]p = .001.

proximately three-fourths of the decline can be attributed to the weakening of partisan loyalties and the reduced feeling of political efficacy.[6] But the changing age distribution of the electorate has also been important.[7] However, the upgrading of educational attainment, income, and occupational status has had a positive effect on voting turnout.[8] Younger citizens have become a larger proportion of the electorate in recent years, and they are much less likely to vote than are older persons (see Tables 7-2 and 7-4). At the same time, the legal environment within which elections are held has changed dramatically, and the barriers to voting that were created by burdensome systems of registration tended to impede voting more among those who were more mobile (and younger citizens move more frequently) and among those who were less psychologically involved in politics, as well as among those for whom political participation was a "luxury" item.[9]

The political environment has also changed. The decline in party identification has been paralleled by an increasing emphasis on the characteristics of the candidates.[10] Among incumbents, it has led to an increased focus on providing services to constituents.[11]

The role of changes in political trust in accounting for declining turnout is in dispute. One view is that the increase in political distrust reflects a decline in support for political institutions, especially by citizens with relatively extreme preferences on major policy issues. The distrustful appear to be polarized into two groups—those on the left, who support policies promoting social change, and those on the right, who prefer a less activist government and a reversal of many welfare-state policies. Both are more likely than others to feel alienated from the system. The dissatisfaction applies to both Republican and Democratic administrations, but it is more prevalent among citizens whose party does not control the government.[12]

A different interpretation is that the political-trust scale used in studies of the electorate measures not citizens' support of political institutions but their evaluations of those who currently hold public office.[13] If the scale measured decline in the support for institutions, those who are less trusting would be less likely to vote and more likely to engage in protest activities.[14] However, the evidence does not support these predictions. While disagreement with current government policies may lead to feelings of political distrust (as measured by the CPS scale items), it does not necessarily result in a decline in support for political institutions, a decline in turnout, or an increase in the use of unconventional forms of political participation (see Table 7-1).

Still another view of political trust is that it is a function of citizens' perceptions of public officials' "intentions, capabilities, and values"—that is, of their trustworthiness and their competence.[15] If citizens vote instrumentally, they weigh the perceived differences among candidates on policies of interest to them by the perceived trustworthiness and competence of the candidates. If a candidate could not be counted on to attempt to put into effect promised policies, or if the candidate were perceived as not being competent to do so, the costs of voting would be seen as outweighing the returns. From this point of view, political trust is related both to voter turnout and to the choices among candidates. Citizens who perceive one candidate as more trustworthy and competent than another are more likely to participate in the election and to vote for the candidate evaluated more favorably on this dimension, if that candidate's policy commitments are also preferred.[16]

Some of these factors appear to have affected turnout in all three midterm elections of the 1970s, while others affected turnout in some midterm elections but not others.[17] The inconsistency of the effects is perhaps not surprising, since different stimuli are presented by any one election, and individuals react differently to the stimuli that are presented. Yet persons with higher education and older persons (those born in 1942 and earlier) were more likely to vote in all of the midterm elections in the 1970s and 1980s. Turnout among high-school- and college-educated individuals increased in 1982 but declined again in 1986. Voters with high levels of education were more likely to vote in 1970 and 1978, but turnout among all educational groups except the lowest dropped in 1974. The political environment in 1974 included recovery from a severe recession and the Watergate scandal, which culminated in that year with President Nixon's resignation and his pardon by President Ford. Evidence for the impact of the recession is provided by the fact that individuals' concern with their future economic well-being affected turnout in the 1974 election but not in the 1970 and 1978 elections, which were not held in the aftermath of a recession.

Examining turnout by different income groups, those who

earn more are more likely to vote, with 60 percent of those in the highest third in income distribution voting, while 54 percent or less of those in the lowest third vote. In 1982, turnout increased among three of the five income groups, perhaps reflecting a reaction to the economic consequences of the recession occurring during the pre-election period, but in 1986 turnout declined among all income groups.

Other political-environment variables did not have the impact that might be expected in the midterm elections of the 1970s. The fact that an election for governor was being held at the same time did not increase the turnout rate. The degree of competition in the gubernatorial contest, the perceived closeness of the contest, and the estimated impact of the alternative outcomes of the election are probably more important than the mere presence or absence of such a contest in stimulating turnout. Higher levels of spending by Democratic congressional candidates were associated with higher turnout, but higher levels of spending by their Republican opponents were not. That probably reflects the usually lower turnout rate of Democratic partisans (see Table 7-3); there was more room for spending by Democratic candidates to have an effect on their partisans. Another political-environment variable related to turnout is region of the country: Citizens residing in the South have been less likely to vote than nonsoutherners.

One indicator of the legal environment, the minimum residence requirement imposed by a state, had an impact on turnout in the 1970 election but not in later elections. By 1974, court decisions and changes in state law had effectively removed lengthy residence requirements.

Strength of partisan identification did not influence turnout in 1974 when the effects of other variables are taken into account, although its effect held up in the other midterm elections. Similarly, when the effects of other variables are taken into account, political efficacy stimulated turnout in 1974 and 1978 but not in 1970. In contrast, caring about the outcome of the election appeared to be important in influencing turnout in all three midterm elections even when other variables were controlled.

Ruy Teixeira, using a set of demographic variables and the

political variables of partisanship, patterns of reading political news in newspapers, and political efficacy, accounted for approximately three-fourths of the variation in voting turnout in presidential elections between 1960 and 1980. Many changes occurred in the sociodemographic characteristics of the electorate during those two decades, including a greater proportion of the electorate attaining higher levels of education and a greater proportion employed in higher status occupations and having higher levels of income. These changes would lead us to expect higher levels of voting turnout, but that did not occur. From 1960 to 1968, changes in sociodemographic variables had less effect on turnout levels than did the decline in feelings of political efficacy. After 1968, increased levels of educational attainment contributed to a significant upward effect on turnout levels. However, demographic variables other than those of socioeconomic status—most important the changed age distribution of the electorate and the decline in newspaper reading—are credited with being the most significant contributors to the decline in voting turnout between 1968 and 1980. Teixeira asserts that the decline in reading about politics in newspapers was the most important variable during the 1968 to 1980; he interprets this as reflecting citizens' decreased involvement in the campaign and lower perceived stakes in electoral outcomes.[18]

Considering the presidential elections from 1960 to the present and the congressional elections in the 1970s, how well do all the explanatory variables together account for the patterns of turnout? The methods and models used by different researchers vary, but one model was able to place survey respondents correctly in the categories of voter and nonvoter approximately 70 percent of the time.[19]

Primary elections to nominate each party's candidate for elective office have received less attention. Earlier research suggested that participants in primaries were atypical of the general electorate.[20] An analysis of 1980 presidential primary-election participants found strength of partisan identification to be important in explaining voting turnout among Democratic party supporters but not among Republican supporters. Political-context variables, such as the number of candidates running in the presidential primary contest, the type of primary, and the perceived closeness of the national contest, were important in explaining participation in Republican presidential primaries. Participation in the Democratic party's primaries was more a function of the personal characteristics of the citizens (those who were older, of majority race, and urban dwellers were more likely to vote), the nature of the primary (turnout is higher in primaries that actually pick delegates), and the presence of a congressional primary at the same time as the presidential primary.[21]

Accounting for Other Forms of Participation

In the effort to explain patterns of participation in political activities other than voting (for a discussion of these kinds of activities, see Chapter 6), one psychological variable that may be important is the individual's values—specifically, the relative weight of material and nonmaterial values. Those emphasizing material values give greater importance to well-being and physical security, whereas individuals emphasizing nonmaterial values stress such attributes as participation in the making of important decisions and aesthetic considerations, which may be reflected in such issues as environmental quality and "humanitarian concerns."

Research in both the United States and Europe suggests that those who emphasize nonmaterial values are more likely to engage in nonvoting forms of participation.[22] It is also possible that the more deeply people hold their values, the more likely they are to participate, whether the values are material or nonmaterial. However, no measure of the depth of commitment to particular values is available.

Only a few studies have examined participation in and support for unconventional political activity in the United States, and hardly any of them have been based on data from national samples. More research has been conducted in other countries, where unconventional participation occurs more often.[23] One explanation for this type of participation focuses on historical factors, such as the timing and rapidity of industrialization and its accompanying social mobilization. Other explanations focus on the political context in which unconventional political behavior occurs, emphasizing the importance of mediating institutions, such as political parties, interest groups, and political movements, in channeling and serving as a vehicle for discontent. Those societies in which such mediating institutions are more widely available tend to have a lower incidence of unconventional political behavior.[24] Indicators of life experiences, such as age, social class, and education, have been used—sometimes in combination with measures of attitudes and beliefs—to account both for participation by the mass public in unconventional political activities and for the genesis of leadership for such activities.[25]

One study of a national sample of U.S. citizens examined the relative importance of five variables in accounting for support for ten different types of protest activities, ranging from signing petitions to damaging property and engaging in personal violence. Of the five variables, age was the most important, though ideological conceptualization, educational level, and material vs. nonmaterial values also made some contribution. The fifth variable, income, appeared to play no part.[26]

Other approaches to unconventional political behavior attribute it to such processes as natural selection, with only the more aggressive of the species surviving, or to an innate passion for territory or space.[27] The validity and reliability of these psychobiological explanations have not yet been established.

Still another approach emphasizes personality traits, such as the needs for survival and security, affection, self-esteem, and self-actualization. However, need variables by themselves are inadequate to explain why some individuals choose to satisfy their needs through unconventional behavior while others choose conventional ways.[28] Other psychological theories focus on a particular personality type, such as the authoritarian personality.[29] Criticisms of these personality-based theories emphasize problems pertaining to the reliability and validity of the measures employed and the biased samples used in the studies employing them.[30] Furthermore, the full range of personality traits that might account for conventional political behavior has not been examined in a comprehensive, systematic fashion.

One well-known theory has suggested that aggressive political behavior is a function of frustration. One component of this theory focuses on an individual's sense of *relative deprivation*, which is defined as a belief that one has not received a rightful share of material goods and/or nonmaterial goods, such as status or a healthful environment. Theories encompassing relative deprivation may also incorporate an examination of the factors that contribute to creating or increasing it.[31] Critics of frustration-aggression theory point out that it fails to explain under what conditions frustration will be expressed as unconventional political behavior and under what conditions it will be expressed in some other way. Furthermore, research has provided evidence undermining the theory itself.[32]

Participation in unconventional forms of political behavior has been viewed by some scholars as a consequence of alienation (see Chapter 3). However, alienation, like frustration, can be expressed in many different types of behavior.

Summary

Trends in voter turnout reflect changes in the electorate's demographic characteristics, such as the increased proportion of younger voters. These trends are also related to declines in the strength of partisanship and political efficacy, as well as to shifts in patterns of partisanship. While it is generally agreed that these changes have contributed to the decline in turnout, researchers do not agree on the effects of changes in political trust. On the other hand, it is clear that changes in the legal environment have made it easier for citizens to register and vote, and these changes, together with rising educational levels, have worked to offset some of the forces tending toward lower turnout.

Other forms of political participation have received less attention from researchers than has voting. A major reason for this is the absence of satisfactory measures of these other forms. The studies that are available, however, suggest that participation in political activities other than voting varies significantly with age and educational attainment. Value differences also affect it, since those for whom nonmaterial values are relatively important are more likely to participate in both conventional and unconventional political activities. The variety and strength of mediating institutions also affect the extent of these nonvoting kinds of participation.

NOTES

1. Most studies have relied upon data obtained through surveys conducted by the Center for Political Studies (CPS) of the University of Michigan. The CPS surveys focus on attitudes and beliefs but also collect information relative to life experience indicators, and more recent studies have added information about the political context of the election contests. The surveys concentrate especially on aspects of the vote choice, including reported voter turnout and campaign activity. Some of the surveys have also included questions about unconventional political participation, and the 1976 survey included measures of other forms of political activity oriented toward both the local and the national political arenas. The Bureau of the Census also conducts surveys after each election to obtain information about voter registration and turnout, but only a few life-experience indicators are included in its data.

2. Results of voter-validation studies are reported in Aage Clausen, "Response Validity: Vote Report," *Public Opinion Quarterly* 32 (1968): 588–606; and Michael W. Traugott and John P. Katosh, "Response Validity in Surveys of Voting Behavior," *Public Opinion Quarterly* 43 (1979): 355–377.

3. John P. Katosh and Michael W. Traugott, "The Consequences of Validated and Self-Reported Voting Measures," *Public Opinion Quarterly* 45 (1981): 519–535. See also Paul R. Abramson and William H. Claggett, "Race-Related Differences in Self-Reported and Validated Turnout," *Journal of Politics* 46 (1984): 719–738; Paul R. Abramson and William Claggett, "Race-Related Differences in Self-Reported and Validated Turnout in 1984," *Journal of Politics* 48 (1986): 412–422; Paul R. Abramson and William Claggett, "Race-Related Differences in Self-Reported and Validated Turnout in 1986," *Journal of Politics* 51 (1989): 397–408.

4. See, for example, Paul R. Abramson and John H. Aldrich, "The Decline of Electoral Participation in America," *American Political Science Review* 76 (1982): 502–521; and Jeffrey A. Smith, *American Presidential Elections: Trust and the Rational Voter* (New York: Praeger, 1980).

5. Howard L. Reiter, "Why Is Turnout Down?" *Public Opinion Quarterly* 43 (1979): 297–311; Stephen D. Shaffer, "A Multivariate Explanation of Decreasing Turnout in Presidential Elections, 1960–1976," *American Journal of Political Science* 25 (1981): 68–95; Raymond E. Wolfinger and Steven J. Rosenstone, *Who Votes?* (New Haven: Yale University Press, 1980); M. Margaret Conway, "Political Participation in Midterm Congressional Elections: Attitudinal and Social Characteristics during the 1970s," *American Politics Quarterly* 9 (1981): 221–244; Carol A. Cassel and David B. Hill, "Explanations of Turnout Decline: A Multivariate Test," *American Politics Quarterly* 9 (1981): 181–196; Gregory Caldeira, Samuel Patterson, and Gregory Markko, "The Mobilization of Voters in Congressional Elections," *Journal of Politics* 47 (1985): 490–509; Lee Sigelman, Philip W. Roeder, Malcolm E. Jewell, and Michael Baer, "Voting and Non-voting: A Multi-election Perspective," *American Journal of Political Science* 29 (1985): 749–765; Ruy Teixeira, *Why Americans Don't Vote: Turnout Decline in the United States 1960–1984* (Westport, Conn.: Greenwood Press, 1987).

6. Abramson and Aldrich, "Decline"; and Paul Keppner, *Who Voted?* (New York: Praeger, 1982), 517. See also the references in the preceding note.

7. Shaffer, "Decreasing Turnout."

8. Teixeira, *Why Americans Don't Vote.*

9. Wolfinger and Rosenstone, *Who Votes?*, chaps. 3 and 5.

10. Smith, *Presidential Elections*, 90–91 and 104–109. However, Weisberg and

Grofman report research indicating that candidate-related factors have little effect on turnout: Herbert F. Weisberg and Bernard Grofman, "Candidate Evaluations and Turnout," *American Politics Quarterly* 9 (1981): 197–219.

11. See, for example, Morris Fiorina, *Congress: Keystone of the Washington Establishment* (New Haven: Yale University Press, 1977), 56–62.

12. Arthur H. Miller, "Political Issues and Trust in Government: 1964–1970," *American Political Science Review* 68 (1974): 951–972.

13. Jack Citrin, "Comment: The Political Relevance of Trust in Government," *American Political Science Review* 68 (1974): 973–989.

14. Citrin, "Comment"; David O. Sears and John McConahay, *The Politics of Violence* (Boston: Houghton Mifflin, 1973); and David C. Schwartz, *Political Alienation and Political Behavior* (Chicago: Aldine, 1973).

15. Smith, *Presidential Elections*, 148. Those who are more trusting are more likely to vote for incumbents in presidential elections and to vote for candidates of the party controlling the White House in midterm congressional elections. See Paul R. Abramson, *Political Attitudes in America* (San Francisco: W. H. Freeman, 1983), 199–200.

16. Abramson, *Political Attitudes*, chaps. 6 and 7.

17. The discussion that follows is based on Conway, "Midterm Congressional Elections."

18. Teixeira, *Why Americans Don't Vote*, chaps. 5 and 6.

19. One criterion for evaluating various models is the amount of variance in the dependent variable, which is explained by the set of independent variables. This is summarized by the statistic R^2. The larger the proportion of variance explained, the higher is the value of R^2, with the maximum value being 1. The R^2 values for several models using variables discussed here (and the method used to estimate those values) are: Smith, *Presidential Elections*—$R^2 = .52$ for 1972 and .37 for 1976 (probit analysis); Conway, "Midterm Congressional Elections"—$R^2 = .24$ for 1970, .43 for 1974, and .33 for 1978 (probit analysis); Shaffer, "Decreasing Turnout"—$R^2 = .15$ for 1960, .12 for 1964, .19 for 1968, .14 for 1972, and .17 for 1976. Abramson and Aldrich, "Decline," in a model that takes advantage of all the data from 1960 to 1980 and includes time as an independent variable, estimate (using regression analysis) that 70 percent of the decline in turnout was due to the decline in party identification and political efficacy. For a discussion of this model, see David B. Hill and Carol A. Cassel, "Comment on Abramson and Aldrich," *American Political Science Review* 77 (1983): 1011–1012; and Paul Abramson and John Aldrich, "Reply to Hill and Cassel," *American Political Science Review* 78 (1984): 792–794.

20. Austin Ranney, "Turnout and Representativeness in Presidential Primary Elections," *American Political Science Review* 66 (1972): 21–47; James I. Lengle, Representation and Presidential Primaries: The Democratic Party in the Post-Reform Era (Westport, Conn.: Greenwood Press, 1981).

21. Barbara Norrander, "Selective Participation: Presidential Primary Voters as a Subset of General Election Voters," *American Politics Quarterly* 14 (1986): 35–53.

22. Ronald Inglehart, "Political Action: The Impact of Values, Cognitive Level, and Social Background," in *Political Action*, ed. Samuel H. Barnes and Max Kaase (Beverly Hills: Sage, 1979), 343–380; Ronald Inglehart, "Post-Materialism in an Environment of Insecurity," *American Political Science Review* 75 (1981): 880–900; Alan Marsh, *Protest and Political Consciousness* (Beverly Hills: Sage, 1977); and Milton Rokeach, *The Nature of Human Values* (New York: Free Press, 1973). See also Edward N. Muller and Karl-Dieter Opp, "Rational Choice and Rebellious Collective Action," *American Political Science Review* 80 (1986): 471–487; and Edward N. Mueller and Mitchell A. Seligson, "Inequality and Insurgency," *American Political Science Review* 81 (1987): 425–451.

23. For a general overview of research on unconventional forms of political participation, see Robert W. Hunt and M. L. Goel, "Unconventional Political Participation," in *Participation in Social and Political Activities*, ed. David Horton Smith, Jacqueline Macauley, and associates (San Francisco: Jossey-Bass, 1980), 133–152.

24. See, for example, Samuel P. Huntington and Joan M. Nelson, *No Easy Choice* (Cambridge: Harvard University Press, 1976); and Samuel P. Huntington, *Political Order in Developing Societies* (New Haven: Yale University Press, 1968).

25. Ted R. Gurr, *Why Men Rebel* (Princeton: Princeton University Press, 1970); Kenneth Keniston, *Young Radicals: Notes on Committed Youth* (New York: Harcourt Brace Jovanovich, 1971); Mancur Olson, Jr., "Rapid Growth as a Destabilizing Force," *Journal of Economic History* 23 (1963): 529–552; I. K. Fierabend and R. L. Fierabend, "Aggressive Behaviors within Politics, 1948–1962: A Cross-National Study," *Journal of Conflict Resolution* 10 (1966): 249–275.

26. *Ideological conceptualization* refers to the level of abstraction at which people think about politics. For example, some people think about politics in terms of "good times" or "bad times," while others, at a higher level of abstraction, evaluate issue positions in terms of the extent to which they are consistent with a preferred ideology, such as liberalism or conservatism. The research is contained in Inglehart, "Political Action." The R^2 for the model for the United States is .27. For a model of participation in illegal political activity using data collected in West Germany, see Edward N. Muller, *Aggressive Political Participation* (Princeton: Princeton University Press, 1979); and Edward N. Muller, "An Explanatory Model for Differing Types of Participation," *European Journal of Political Research* 10 (1982): 1–16.

27. Konrad Lorenz, *On Aggression* (New York: Bantam, 1967); and Robert Ardrey, *The Territorial Imperative* (New York: Atheneum, 1966).

28. For research on need satisfaction and political behavior, see Jeanne N. Knutson, *The Human Basis of the Polity* (Chicago: Aldine-Atherton, 1972).

29. Theodor W. Adorno, Else Frankel-Brunswik, Daniel J. Levinson, and R. Nevitt Sanford, *The Authoritarian Personality* (New York: Harper and Row, 1950); J. P. Kirscht and R. C. Dillehay, *Dimensions of Authoritarianism* (Lexington: University of Kentucky Press, 1963).

30. Richard Christie and Marie Jahoda (eds.), *Studies in the Scope and Method of "The Authoritarian Personality"* (Glencoe, Ill.: Free Press, 1954).

31. For the major formulation of frustration-aggression theory, see John Dollard, Leonard Doob, Neal Miller, O. H. Mowrer, and Robert R. Sears, *Frustration and Aggression* (New Haven: Yale University Press, 1939).

32. For a critique of the frustration-aggression theory, see Leonard Berkowitz, "The Frustration-Aggression Hypothesis Revisited: Some Implications of Laboratory Studies of Frustration and Aggression," *American Behavioral Scientist* 11 (1968): 14–19.

Chapter 8

Does Political Participation
Make a Difference?

The assumption underlying any discussion of political participation is that political participation makes a difference.
However, it is possible that political participation is merely symbolic, enhancing participants' sense of affection for and commitment to the political system and conferring legitimacy on
political leaders and their actions. Alternatively, political participation may have instrumental effects, influencing those who participate, the selection of leaders and choice of policies, and the
operations of the political system. This chapter considers whether
political participation does have instrumental effects. Three possible types of effects are examined: effects on the individual who
engages in political participation, on the representation of citizens in the governing process, and on the products of the political system—its policy outputs and the outcomes for the citizens
that result from those policies.

Effects of Participation on the Individual

Much of the recent theorizing on political participation in
democracies has seen it as a means of controlling those who
govern. That view has been summarized by Pateman in this fashion:

Elections are crucial to the democratic method for it is primarily
through elections that the majority can exercise control over their leaders. Responsiveness of leaders to non-elite demands, or "control" over
leaders, is ensured primarily through the sanction of loss of office at

elections; the decisions of leaders can also be influenced by active groups bringing pressure to bear during inter-election periods. "Political equality" in the theory refers to universal suffrage and to the existence of equality of opportunity of access to channels of influence over leaders. . . . "participation," so far as the majority is concerned, is participation in the choice of decision makers. Therefore, the function of participation in the theory is solely a protective one.[1]

Critics of this view argue that participation is important because of its effects on the quality of life for the individual participant. Therefore, participation in a democracy should accomplish more than acting as citizens' control over decision making by deciding "who governs."

If there is to be participatory democracy at all, the mere presence of representative institutions is not sufficient. Democracy requires participation, and participation cannot be fostered by political institutions alone. Pateman asserts that "the major function of participation in the theory of participatory democracy is . . . an educative one . . . including both the psychological aspect and the gaining of practice in democratic skills and procedures." She continues:

For a democratic society to exist it is necessary for a participatory society to exist, i.e., a society where all political systems have been democratised and socialization through participation can take place in all areas.[2]

In participatory theory, participation means "equal participation in the making of decisions" and political equality means equal power in determining political outcomes. The result of participation is not only that a certain type of political decision and policy outcome occurs, but also that the fulfillment of the human potential of all citizens is maximized. In other words, political participation is necessary to achieve the satisfaction of the highest need in Maslow's hierarchy of needs—the need for self-actualization.[3]

One inference to be drawn from this line of argument is that participation in other types of activity will lead to higher levels of political participation than would otherwise be expected and that, conversely, political participation will lead to participation in decision making in a wider variety of situations than just deciding "who governs." Another inference is that political participation should lead to an enhanced sense of political efficacy, greater interest in public affairs, and a greater sense of involvement in and commitment to the political system. What is implied is a reciprocal relationship, with greater participation in decision making involving the family, school, and employment leading to greater involvement with and participation in politics, which in turn feeds back into greater involvement in nonpolitical decision making. More positive attitudes and beliefs about the self, others, and society would follow.

If these inferences are correct, early childhood participation in decision making in the family and school would lead to higher levels of political participation in adult life. Later experiences at work or in voluntary organizations, developing a sense of control over one's life and of trust in others, would also contribute to increased political participation.

Some research does provide evidence that other forms of participation foster the attitudes and beliefs that contribute to higher levels of political participation and that political participation leads to greater confidence in one's ability to have an impact on decision making in other arenas. One study used data collected in 1959 and 1960 in five nations—United States, Great Britain, West Germany, Italy, and Mexico—to examine whether individuals who remembered participating in family decisions and school or workplace discussions also believed that they were competent to function effectively in the political system. The proportions reporting have some influence in family decision making ranged from 73 percent in the United States and 69 percent in Great Britain to 57 percent in Mexico. The differences in perceived freedom to participate in school discussions were much greater: While 40 percent of the respondents in the United States said that they had opportunities to do so and actually did, the proportions making the same claim in the other countries were between 16 percent (Great Britain) and 11 percent (Italy).[4] Participation in both areas varied with social class, as measured by level of educational attainment, with those in higher status groups reporting higher rates of participation. Remembered participation also varied with age, with those who were younger being more likely to report participating.

In the workplace, the proportions that reported being often or sometimes consulted about job decisions ranged from 59 percent in Mexico to 78 percent in the United States and 80 percent in Great Britain. Those in higher status occupations were more likely to have been consulted.[5]

The study found that respondents' sense of subjective competence—their confidence in their ability "to appeal to a set of regular and orderly rules in their dealings with administrative officials"—did vary to some extent with their remembered participation in family decision making and school discussions, although the relationship was primarily among those with lower levels of educational attainment and in younger age groups.[6] No relationship exists between reported participation in workplace decision making and sense of competence. (This finding, however, may be a result of the questions used to measure participation in workplace decision making. The questions asked whether the respondents were consulted when decisions were made on the job and also inquired about the extent to which they felt free to protest if a decision they did not like was made and the extent to which they had actually protested when such a decision was made.) The researchers concluded that the transfer of participatory experiences in the family and school to the political system may be conditioned by a set of psychological or social factors that influence both childhood participation in decisions and discussions and participation in decision making as adults.

Several studies that examined the political attitudes of factory employees who enjoyed some autonomy in job-related decisions have reported that higher participatory political orientations were associated with a higher than usual degree of democracy in the workplace and with the resulting quality of job satisfaction.[7] Other research has found that persons who have reached the need-satisfaction stage of "self-actualization" (see Chapter 3) are more likely to participate in politics, but the relationship was weak, and it varied with social class.[8] A study of worker-owners in a forest-industry cooperative reported that they did not exhibit greater cooperative and egalitarian orientations.[9] This may reflect differences between the employee and worker-owner roles in factory decision making.

The discussion so far has dealt with the impact of participation in decision making in other areas of one's life on political orientations and participation. The obverse question is whether participation in some political activities affects subsequent participation in other political activities, attitudes and beliefs about the political system, and orientations toward other arenas of decision making.

One effort to answer this question was made in a study of younger citizens who were first interviewed in 1965, while they were high-school seniors, and were then interviewed again in 1973.[10] Between those years, the Vietnam War disrupted the lives of many citizens, especially those in this age group. A significant number of the men served in the armed forces, and as the war became more and more unpopular, many civilians engaged in protests against it. One goal of the researchers was to ascertain the extent to which participation or nonparticipation in protest against the war affected political attitudes, beliefs, and patterns of participation.

The thesis underlying this part of their analysis was that of Karl Mannheim, who drew a distinction between a "generation as actuality" and "generation-units." A generation as actuality, he hypothesized, is created when individuals of the same age group during a period of social destabilization "participate in the characteristic social and intellectual currents of their society and period, and . . . have an active or passive experience of the interactions of forces which made up the new situation." Members of the generation, however, may react differently to their experiences, resulting in generation-units—"groups within the same actual generation which work up the material or their common experience in different specific ways."[11]

In order to see whether protest participation itself had an effect on later attributes, beliefs, and participation patterns, the study controlled for the 1965 levels of these orientations and patterns. In addition, to eliminate the effects of education, only college graduates were studied. The analysis of the data showed that protest participation between 1965 and 1973 raised the 1973 levels of political knowledge and use of the print-news media, while it decreased political trust and efficacy. Protest participation also affected party identification and strength of identification, and altered positions on such issues as school integration and school prayer. These impacts remained even when the effects of academic major, size of the higher educational institution attended, and type of college or university (public versus private) were removed. Moreover, the effects were greater for those who had engaged in more protests. The protesters also differed from the nonprotesters in their evaluations of various groups. Thus, the Vietnam War appears to have created different generation-units, with those who participated in opposing the war undergoing greater changes in their previous attitudes, beliefs, and participation repertories and also developing different attitudes on newly emerging issues.[12]

Another analysis of data from this study found, rather unexpectedly, that the effects of service in the armed forces during the Vietnam War were "non-existent to negligible."[13] This striking contrast to the effects of protest participation was attributed to the differences in recruitment. Being a protester was a voluntary act, while being in the armed forces was largely a consequence of being drafted or of enlisting as a reaction to the high probability of being drafted. Furthermore, the protesters came from a relatively homogeneous background, while those who served in the military came from varied backgrounds. Attitude crystallization and the reinforcement derived from the experiences also differed, with responses to military service being more varied, attitudes being less crystallized, and responses to experiences being more closely supervised by superior officers. Thus, military service during the Vietnam War failed to result in the creation of a generation-unit.[14]

Participation and Representation

One may also ask whether and how participation affects the character of representation in a democratic polity. The question is complicated by the fact that *representation* is a term with several different meanings. First, it may refer to the resemblance to or reflection of the characteristics of what is represented. This may be called *descriptive representation*. For example, the rules governing the selection of delegates to the 1972 national nominating convention of the Democratic party required that young people, women, and minorities be represented in "reasonable proportion" to their numbers in a state's population. Subsequently, the rules were revised to call for equal numbers of men and women in each state and territorial delegation, but all other requirements for the representation of demographically described groups were dropped (although state party committees were directed to make a "positive effort" to ensure that any Democrat who wished to participate in the delegate selection process would be able to do so). The incongruity of requiring equal representation by gender but not by other demographic categories is evident.[15]

A second type of representation may be called *representation of political views,* in which the attitudes, beliefs, and policy preferences of a constituency are matched by the attitudes, beliefs, and policy preferences of its representative, or at least are matched by the representative's decisions.[16] This is usually interpreted to mean that a legislator votes in accordance with the views of the majority in the represented district. However, defining the "majority" is not always easy. Is it a majority of those who voted in the last election or of those who will vote in the next election? Is it the majority of those who voted in the primary election or the majority of those who voted in the general election? And how does a legislator represent constituents' views when the majority of the electorate has no opinion on an issue, as sometimes happens?

Representation of political views can come about in one of two ways. Either the voters elect a representative who shares their views, or the constituents make their views known to their representative following the election—typically, at the time when the representative is about to vote on some bill. In either case, the views represented are a function of who participates.[17] If half the voters in a district favor allowing formal prayers in schools and half of them oppose it, but two-thirds of those in favor vote while only one-third of those opposed vote, the *effective majority* supports formal prayers. Similarly, if constituents communicate their views to their representative after the election, the views of those who write the letters, make the phone calls, or meet with the representative will have the most influence.

There can be a conflict between descriptive representation and representation of political views.[18] One study found that the delegates to the 1972 Democratic convention, selected under rules that emphasized reflection of demographic characteristics, were less representative of the policy views of Democrats than were the delegates to subsequent conventions, when descriptive representation in terms of demographic categories was no longer required (except, as noted, for gender).[19]

A third concept of representation focuses not on the congruence of views between individual public officials and their constituencies but on the congruence between the distribution of policy preferences among the electorate and in the representative body as a whole. The argument is that congruence need not exist between a particular representative and a particular district as long as the views of that district are represented somewhere in the legislative body.[20] In this approach to representation, emphasis is placed on participatory acts that affect a number of representatives, not just those representing one's own constituency. Actions such as contributing to the campaign committee of some other congressional district's candidate, to a political action committee, or to a party's congressional campaign committee could have significant effects on who serves and what distribution of views is reflected in the institution. That pattern of contributing has become more prominent in recent years in the United States. Again, the distribution of representatives' attitudes, beliefs, and policy preferences will reflect the views of those who in some way contributed to the election of any member of the representative body (or who tried to influence the representatives once they attained the office), not necessarily the views of the total potential electorate.

Using data collected by interviewing samples of House members, their electoral opponents, and their constituents, one study reported an improvement in the representation of views on three issues when considered from an institutional perspective.[21] A later study, based on roll-call data from the 95th Congress (1977–1978) and a sample of representatives and their opponents, came to a similar conclusion, but it also found that if adequacy of representation was evaluated in terms of collective satisfaction with the outcome, then collective representation did not provide greater satisfaction than did representation considered in terms of each individual member's representation of the views of his or her constituency.[22]

A fourth view of representation is that of acting for others or acting on their behalf. A classic statement of this view was presented by Edmund Burke, a member of the British House of Commons in the eighteenth century, who defended the actions of legislators, such as himself, in voting for policies they believed were in the best interest of their constituents even when those policies were not the ones preferred by their constituents.[23] Hanna Pitkin, a latter-day exponent of this view, has said:

The representative must act independently; his action must involve discretion and judgment; he must be the one who acts. The represented must also be (conceived as) capable of independent action and judgment, not merely being taken care of. . . . The representative must act in such a way that there is no conflict, or if it occurs an explanation is called for. He must not be found persistently at odds with the wishes of the represented without good reasons in terms of their interest, without a good explanation of why their wishes are not in accord with their interests.[24]

This perspective on representation also suggests that active participation is necessary. Representatives' perceptions of their constituencies are shaped both by their own prior beliefs and attitudes and by the activities of members of their constituencies.[25]

Participation and Policy Outcomes

A crucial question in the study of participation is what impact it has on policy outcomes. The increased openness of the American political system to participation by young people, minorities, and women has stimulated a number of studies of the descriptive representativeness of holders of various elective and appointive offices. But as already noted, descriptive representation does not necessarily lead to accurate representation of policy preferences or to the election of representatives who act on behalf of their constituents' interests. Indeed, it can be expected that citizens with similar demographic characteristics will have different preferences on many issues. For example, if only because of their other group attachments, not all citizens in the thirty-five-to-fifty-five age group have the same positions on issues such as the level of government financial support for public education or the granting of tax credits for tuition payments by families to private schools.

The passive view of representation underlying descriptive representation makes at least two assumptions. One is that demographic characteristics determine political-socialization experiences. The second is that when differentially socialized individuals have discretion in decision making, their decisions will tend to be of particular benefit to, or particularly in the interest of, members of their demographic group—for example, that black elected officials will favor policies beneficial to blacks when there is an issue that divides blacks and whites, or that female elected officials will tend to favor the position preferred by women when public opinion on an issue differs between men and women. However, on most issues, division along demographic lines is less likely to occur than is division on some other basis, such as a general philosophical view in support of an active government versus a preference for limited governmental activity. Nevertheless, the political strategies pursued by a candidate for elective office frequently must take into account the reaction of groups in the electorate to various aspects of the candidate's hypothetical descriptive representative. For example, when John F. Kennedy, a Catholic, ran for president, the question of whether he would be particularly responsive to the interests and leaders of the Catholic church became a major issue. Kennedy faced that issue in a campaign speech on September 12, 1960, when he said:

I believe in an America where the separation of Church and State is absolute—where no Catholic prelate would tell the President (should he be a Catholic) how to act, and no Protestant minister would tell his parishioners for whom to vote—where no church or church school is granted any public funds or political preference—and where no man is denied public office merely because his religion differs from the President who might appoint him or the people who might elect him.[26]

One way of examining the impact of participation and type of representation on policy outcomes is to track their relationships over time; another is to compare their relationships across jurisdictions that vary in their participation patterns or representational styles. Examples of the first type of analysis are the studies of the impact of black elected and appointed officials. Only recently have black citizens been elected or appointed to public office in substantial numbers in many areas of the United States. Several studies of black mayors in both southern and nonsouthern jurisdictions suggest that their election has had an effect on the policy outputs of city governments.[27] Some research using expenditure patterns as the measure of policy output has concluded that, while the level of black representation on the city council has no effect, the presence of black mayors does make a difference, being associated with greater spending on social welfare and less spending on amenities, physical plant, and—according to some studies—protective services such as fire and police. These effects may vary with the type of city government system (for example, strong versus weak mayor). But gross expenditure patterns may be too crude a measure; the amount spent on public education, for example, may not change, but the expenditures may be more equitably distributed among the schools in the school system. One study has shown that representation of blacks increases the employment of blacks in the state bureaucracy.[28] Black representation on school boards has been found to lead to a reduction of racial differences in some school-system outputs, although this effect is weakened when controls are applied for the level of black resources in the jurisdiction.[29] This last study suggested that a set of conditions could be specified as being necessary for the translation of descriptive representation into policy outcomes:

1. Some members of the group must be in a decision-making position;

2. Some issues must be important to members of the group;

3. These issues must be on the decision-making body's agenda;

4. The group members on the decision-making body must hold the same issue position as the majority or dominant plurality within the group or believe it necessary to act as though they held the same policy preferences;

5. The group's representatives on the decision-making body must be able to influence the decisions made; and

6. The policies adopted must be appropriately implemented.[30]

If one or more of these conditions is not met, as often happens, descriptive representation does not have policy impacts.

In some studies of the relationships among participation, representation, and policy outcomes, surrogate indicators for participation levels are used and the type of representation is simply assumed. For example, studies of voting-participation levels may use the percentage of the voting-age population in a particular category—such as percent female, percent with Spanish surnames, or percent nonwhite—as the measure of participation, but such a measure would be valid only if turnout levels were the same among all groups. That assumption obviously deviates from reality, but estimates of the different turnout rates of groups are not available in many types of elections.

An example of cross-jurisdictional research, which also illustrates the methodological problems frequently involved in this kind of research, is a study of Mississippi state legislators' support for redistributive social welfare policies. The researchers constructed an index of legislators' voting patterns from twenty-eight roll calls held in 1976 and 1977, all of them involving policies that would have shifted benefits to less affluent citizens of Mississippi. They then investigated the relationship between that index and the proportion of the voting-age population that was black in the state's legislative districts. They found that the relationship was curvilinear: support for redistributive policies was high in districts where less than 15 percent of the voting-age population was black, decreased in districts with higher proportions of blacks, reaching its lowest level in districts with 25 to 35 percent black voting-age population, then increased in districts with up to 49.9 percent black, and then decreased again.[31] This puzzling pattern can presumably be explained only by differences in the nature of representation in different types of districts.

The effects of the type of electoral arrangements on descriptive representation have been a subject of controversy and research. For example, does use of district or at-large electoral systems make a difference in who gets elected to city councils, school boards, or state legislatures, or are other factors, such as the education, affluence, and other socioeconomic characteristics of the voters, more important? Some have argued the latter point of view,[32] but there is persuasive evidence that the electoral structure has a significant, perhaps even dominant, impact on the extent of descriptive representation.[33] Other factors that may affect it are the extent of organizational memberships, the strength of the organizations, and the skill of organizational leaders.[34]

As already pointed out, descriptive representation may not result in representation of constituents' preferences or interests. A group's representatives may be reluctant to advocate the group's views, particularly if a majority of the other public officials on the council, commission, or board are not receptive to them.[35] (Of course, even if the group's representatives do share the policy positions of a majority of the group and do advocate them, those positions may not be supported by a majority of the representative body.)

Constituencies influence their representatives' policy choices when either the representatives adopt the policy positions of their constituents or the representatives, although not sharing their constituents' policy preferences, work to promote those preferences by attempting to enact appropriate legislation. One study examined the relationship among constituency preferences in a sample of districts, perceptions of those preferences by the district's congressional representatives, and the representatives' own preference, in three policy areas: civil rights, social welfare, and foreign policy. It provides evidence on the question of the extent of representation as congruence and as acting for the interest of the constituents. There was a relatively high degree of correspondence between constituents' attitudes and representatives' perceptions of those attitudes in the area of civil rights, but a much lower correspondence in the other two areas. The association between the representatives' own attitudes and their constituents' attitudes was weaker still, being moderate for the civil rights policy area, weak for social welfare, and almost zero on foreign policy.[36] Thus, among these three policy areas and at that time (1958), representation by congruence of views could occur only in civil rights, although one might argue that, in the other areas, the representatives' views, while not similar to those of their constituents, were nevertheless in their "best interests," in which case representation would be of the "acting for" type.

The mass public lacks well-informed attitudes on many issues; foreign policy issues are generally less salient to most citizens than are domestic issues, and even within the domestic-policy areas, issues vary in their salience. Citizens also differ in the degree of their concern with the issues that are salient to them. Hence, what may be important for the quality of representation is that those for whom a particular issue is salient and who care most about it are able, through one or more forms of participation, to bring the issue to the attention of their representatives and that the representatives take account of views of this issue in formulating, enacting, and implementing public policy.

Influence over policy is exerted not only by voting but also by many other methods. Through less conventional methods of participation, such as protest marches and demonstrations, issues can be put on the policy agendas of otherwise unreceptive decision makers.[37] Once an issue is on the policy agenda, activities other than voting may indicate to decision makers what the parameters of acceptable decisions are to those who are most concerned with it. For example, those who are active in a campaign can significantly affect the perceptions of others, mobilizing some of them to work for or against a candidate and to participate in other ways in influencing policy outcomes. As the campaign activities of an anti-abortion group against incumbent senators in Iowa in 1978 and 1980 demonstrated, such activities can have a decisive effect on close elections (see Chapter 4). The activities of a passionate minority can make clear to a representative the strategic costs and benefits of pursuing certain policy options, even if these activities do not dictate a specific policy stand.

The impact of participation on policy outcomes can also be assessed in terms of the differences in policy preferences between those who vote and those who do not. During the period from 1952 to the present, voters have tended to be more conservative on economic issues than nonvoters, though the magnitude of the difference has decreased since the later 1960s. On many noneconomic issues—notably, racial, public-order, and life-style concerns—the views of voters and nonvoters are relatively homogeneous. On the other hand, on issues such as housing and social integration, abortion, and women's rights, voters tend to be more liberal than nonvoters.[38] However, in 1984 those opposed to government involvement on several domestic issues were more likely to vote than were those who favored government activity in those policy areas.[39] In 1988, those who favored a more activist government in dealing with the issues of domestic spending, government health insurance, government support for guaranteed jobs, and government aid for minorities were more likely to vote than were individuals who supported more conservative positions on those policies. In contrast, differences in policy preferences on the issues of equal rights for women, defense spending, and Soviet-American relations were not associated with variations in turnout rates.[40]

It is also pertinent to ask whether the problems most important to nonvoters get onto the policy agenda at all. One historian has concluded that the class bias in voting participation

imbalances the operation of the participation-response system, so that the interests of the electorally inactive remain invisible. . . . Persistingly low turnout among working-class citizens relieves elected officeholders of even the likelihood of a retrospective electoral sanction.[41]

Even if the issues relevant to nonvoters are included on the policy agenda, they may not get very much attention.

The American South provides ample evidence of the effects of political and social change on participation patterns; the increase in black political participation in turn has had an impact on the characteristics of representatives and representation and on policy outcomes. The change in the level of black political participation was in part stimulated by federal laws, such as the Civil Rights Act of 1964 and the Voting Rights Act of 1965, both of which contributed to increased participation by racial minorities in the southern states. These laws opened access to political participation for many black citizens previously denied the right to vote, to serve in elected office, or to participate on appointive boards and commissions.

That the opportunity to participate has been used by blacks is demonstrated in voter-registration data. Black registration in the South increased from 29 percent of the black voting-age population in 1960 to 62 percent in 1970[42] and 65 percent in 1986.[43]

To what extent have other means of participation been used, and what have been the effects of participation, whatever the type, on public- and private-sector social and economic policies? James Button's in-depth study of the impact of changes in black political participation on public- and private-sector policies from the late 1950s to the mid-1980s in six southern communities demonstrates that participation patterns can have a significant impact on those policies.[44] However, Button concludes that the effect of participation in stimulating change varies with the nature of the community and the kind of policy. The effects were less in the private sector than in the public, but the presence of black elected officials did have an impact on private-sector employment. Collective action by blacks, such as protest demonstrations, boycotts, and sit-ins, had a significant impact on employment patterns in the 1960s and a lesser impact in the 1970s. While the extent and effects of black participation varied with the community context, such as size of place, proportion of blacks in the community, and political culture (Old South versus New South), Button concludes that black political participation contributed to gains in political power, but that improvements in social and economic conditions have been "more difficult and less apparent."[45] While levels of municipal services improved significantly as a result of increased participation, the degree of improvement varied with the type of community and the kind of municipal service.[46]

Evidence that the southern electorate has changed significantly as a consequence of both increased black political participation and other changes (increased urbanization and the development of an urban middle class, generational replacement, and increased employment of women outside the home) is also provided by Earl Black and Merle Black in *Politics and Society in the South*. However, their assessment of public policy concludes that while southern state governments provide more services than in the past,

as a rule they tax lightly, regulate mainly where the public interest is so compelling that governmental intervention cannot be avoided, and spend comparatively little except where there are unmistakable direct benefits for the middle and upper-middle classes. In general, southern governments give scant attention and few tangible benefits to those in the bottom half of the social structure.[47]

The impact of increased black participation in southern politics appears to vary with the level of government and, within each level, with a host of factors, such as the proportion of the electorate that is black and the type of dominant political culture.

Summary

The evidence considered in this chapter suggests that participation, whether it is in the political or nonpolitical areas of life, tends to influence individuals' attitudes and beliefs in the direction of more positive orientations toward both themselves and the political system. Patterns of participation also affect the representation of citizens' views in the political system. Representation can occur in the form of descriptive representation, or as the congruence in policy preferences between a representative and the members of the representative's constituency, or through the representative's acting on behalf of those who are represented. Participation in all its forms has impacts both on what is put on the policy agenda and on the outcomes that occur as a result of governmental decision making.

The effectiveness of participation cannot be inferred just from the numbers who participate. Effectiveness is also dependent on both the quality of the participatory activity and the context within which the participation occurs. Indeed, one of the necessary conditions for policy impact may be to change the context, such as replacing those who serve in elected office to ensure a greater receptiveness to the policy demands of those who are represented.

NOTES

1. Carole Pateman, *Participation and Democratic Theory* (Cambridge: Cambridge University Press, 1970), 14.
2. Ibid., 42–43.
3. Abraham Maslow, "A Theory of Human Motivation," *Psychological Review* 50 (1943): 370–396.
4. Gabriel A. Almond and Sidney Verba, *The Civic Culture: Political Attitudes and Democracy in Five Nations* (Princeton: Princeton University Press, 1963), 330–332.
5. Ibid., 331, table 3.
6. Ibid., 217 and 346–355.
7. J. Maxwell Elden, "Political Efficacy at Work: The Connection between More Autonomous Forms of Workforce Organization and a More Participatory Politics," *American Political Science Review* 75 (1981): 43–58; Harold Sheppard and Neal Herrick, *Where Have All the Robots Gone?* (New York: Free Press, 1972); and William C. Torbet and Malcolm Rogers, *Being for the Most Part Puppets* (Cambridge, Mass.: Schenkman, 1972).
8. Jeanne Knutson, *The Human Basis of the Polity* (Chicago: Aldine-Atherton, 1972), 236, table 4.50, and 342, appendix D, part 1.
9. Edward Greenberg, "Industrial Self-Management and Political Attitudes," *American Political Science Review* 75 (1981): 29–42.
10. M. Kent Jennings and Richard Niemi, *Generations and Politics* (Princeton: Princeton University Press, 1981).
11. Karl Mannheim, "The Problem of Generations," in *The New Pilgrims*, ed. Philip Altbach and Robert S. Laufer (New York: David McKay, 1972), 119–120.
12. Jennings and Niemi, *Generations and Politics*, chap. 11.
13. M. Kent Jennings and Gregory B. Markus, "The Effects of Military Service on Political Attitudes: A Panel Study," *American Political Science Review* 71 (1977): 131–147; and Jennings and Niemi, *Generations and Politics*, 378–379.
14. Jennings and Niemi, *Generations and Politics*, 378–379. Differences might be found between those who served in Vietnam and those who did not, or between those who served in combat units in Vietnam and those who served in support units, but the sample is too small to permit analysis of the effects of patterns of service in Vietnam.
15. David E. Price, *Bring Back the Parties* (Washington, D.C.: CQ Press, 1984), 231–232. For a more sanguine view of the consequences of reform, see William Crotty, *Party Reform* (New York: Longman, 1983).
16. Heinz Eulau and Paul D. Karps, "The Puzzle of Representation: Specifying Components of Responsiveness," *Legislative Studies Quarterly* 2 (1977): 233–254.
17. Aage Clausen, *How Congressmen Decide: A Policy Focus* (New York: St. Martin's, 1973), 131–133. Which party the representative is from or who the

particular representative is makes a difference. Patterns of roll-call votes differ even when a change in representative results only in a different person from the same party being elected. See ibid., chap. 6; and Lewis A. Froman, Jr., *Congressmen and Their Constituencies* (Chicago: Rand McNally, 1963), chap. 4.

18. Austin Ranney, *Curing the Mischiefs of Faction* (Berkeley and Los Angeles: University of California Press, 1975), 111–115; and Jeane Kirkpatrick, *The New Presidential Elite* (New York: Russell Sage Foundation and Twentieth Century Fund, 1976), chap. 10. See also John S. Jackson III, J. C. Brown, and Barbara Leavitt Brown, "Recruitment, Representation, and Political Values: The 1976 Democratic National Convention Delegates," *American Politics Quarterly* 6 (1978): 187–212; and John S. Jackson III, Barbara Leavitt Brown, and David Bositis, "Herbert McClosky and Friends Revisited: 1980 Democratic and Republican Elites Compared to the Mass Public," *American Politics Quarterly* 10 (1982): 158–180.

19. Kirkpatrick, *Presidential Elite*, chap. 10.

20. Robert Weisberg, "Collective vs. Dyadic Representation," *American Political Science Review* 72 (1978): 535–547.

21. Ibid., 541, table 3.

22. Patricia A. Hurley, "Collective Representation Reappraised," *Legislative Studies Quarterly* 7 (1982): 119–136.

23. Edmund Burke, "Speech to the Electors of Bristol at the Conclusion of the Poll, 3 November 1774," in *Selected Prose of Edmund Burke*, ed. Philip Magnus (London: Falcon Press, 1948), 29–31.

24. Hannah Pitkin, *The Concept of Representation* (Berkeley: University of California Press, 1967), 209–210.

25. For reviews of research on representative institutions relating to legislative-constituency connections, see Melissa P. Collie, "Voting Behavior in Legislatures," *Legislative Studies Quarterly* 9 (1984): 3–50; Malcolm Jewell, "Legislative Constituency Relations and the Representative Process," *Legislative Studies Quarterly* 8 (1983): 303–338; Lyn Ragsdale, "Responsiveness and Legislative Elections: Toward a Comparative Study," *Legislative Studies Quarterly* 8 (1983): 339–379; and Eric M. Uslaner, "Legislative Behavior: The Study of Representation," in *Political Behavior I*, ed. Samuel Long (Boulder, Colo.: Westview, 1984). For studies of the characteristics of constituency-representative relationships, see the studies cited in those works, and Richard F. Fenno, Jr., *Home Style: House Members in Their Districts* (Boston: Little, Brown, 1978); David R. Mayhew, *Congress: The Electoral Connection* (New Haven: Yale University Press, 1974); Morris P. Fiorina, *Congress: Keystone of the Washington Establishment* (New Haven: Yale University Press, 1977), chap. 4; and Morris P. Fiorina, *Representatives, Roll Calls, and Constituencies* (Lexington, Mass.: Lexington Books, 1974).

26. Quoted in Theodore H. White, *The Making of the President, 1960* (New York: Atheneum, 1961), 260.

27. David Campbell and Joe R. Feagin, "Black Politics in the South: A Descriptive Analysis," *Journal of Politics* 37 (1975): 129–159; William R. Keech, *The Impact of Negro Voting* (Chicago: Rand McNally, 1968); Charles H. Levine, *Racial Conflicts and the American Mayor* (Lexington, Mass.: Lexington Books, 1974); W. Nelson and P. Meranto, *Electing Black Mayors* (Columbus: Ohio State University Press, 1976); Chuck Stone, *Black Political Power in America* (New York: Dell, 1971); and Susan Welch and Albert K. Karnig, *Black Representation and Urban Policy* (Chicago: University of Chicago Press, 1980).

28. Kenneth J. Meier, "Affirmative Action: Constraints and Policy Impact," in *Race, Sex, and Policy Problems*, ed. Marian L. Palley and Michael B. Preston (Lexington, Mass.: Lexington Books, 1979).

29. Kenneth J. Meier and Robert F. England, "Black Representation and Educational Policy: Are They Related?" *American Political Science Review* 78 (1984): 392–403.

30. These are generalized from Meier and England, "Black Representation and Educational Policy."

31. Charles S. Bullock III and Susan A. MacManus, "Policy Responsiveness to the Black Electorate," *American Politics Quarterly* 9 (1981): 357–368; see especially 360–361. For discussions of district characteristics and legislative voting patterns at the national level, see Michael W. Combs, John R. Hibbing, and Susan Welch, "Black Constituents and Congressional Roll Call Votes," *Western Political Quarterly* 37 (1984): 424–434; and Charles S. Bullock III, "Congressional Voting and the Mobilization of a Black Electorate in the South," *Journal of Politics* 43 (1981): 662–682.

32. Leonard Cole, "Electing Blacks to Municipal Office: Structural and Social Determinants," *Urban Affairs Quarterly* 10 (1974): 17–39; Susan A. MacManus, "City Council Election Procedures and Minority Representation: Are They Related?" *Social Science Quarterly* 59 (1978): 153–161; and Albert K. Karnig, "Black Resources and City Council Representation," *Journal of Politics* 41 (1979): 134–139.

33. Richard L. Engstrom and Michael D. MacDonald, "The Election of Blacks to City Councils: Clarifying the Impact of Electoral Arrangements on the Seats/Population Relationships," *American Political Science Review* 75 (1981): 344–355; Keech, *Negro Voting*; and Albert Karnig, "Black Representation on City Councils: The Impact of District Election and Socio-Economic Factors," *Urban Affairs Quarterly* 12 (1976): 223–256.

34. Keech, *Negro Voting*; Donald Matthews and James Prothro, *Negroes and the New Southern Politics* (New York: Harcourt, Brace and World, 1966), chaps. 7 and 8; and Meier, "Affirmative Action: Constraints and Policy Impacts."

35. Keech, *Negro Voting*.

36. Warren E. Miller and Donald E. Stokes, "Constituency Influence in Congress," *American Political Science Review* 57 (1963): 45–56. For a reanalysis of the data pertaining to civil rights, see Charles F. Cnudde and Donald J. McCrone, "The Linkage between Constituency Attitudes and Congressional Voting Behavior: A Causal Model," *American Political Science Review* 60 (1966): 66–72.

37. For a discussion of the effectiveness of protest marches and demonstrations in forcing a southern city to deal with certain issues in the early and mid-1960s, see Keech, *Negro Voting*, 83–87.

38. Stephen D. Shaffer, "Policy Differences between Voters and Non-Voters in American Elections," *Western Political Quarterly* 35 (1982): 496–510. See also Raymond E. Wolfinger and Steven J. Rosenstone, *Who Votes?* (New Haven: Yale University Press, 1980), 111; and Paul R. Abramson, John H. Aldrich, and David Rohde, *Change and Continuity in the 1980 Elections* (Washington, D.C.: CQ Press, 1982), 89. The conclusion of these books is that voters and nonvoters did not differ significantly in their policy preferences in the 1972 and 1980 elections, respectively. In a study of a Wisconsin primary, Ranney found that nonvoters differed from voters on only two of twenty-one issues: Austin Ranney, "The Representativeness of Primary Electorates," *Midwest Journal of Political Science* 12 (1968): 224–238. See also Austin Ranney and Leon Epstein, "The Two Electorates: Voters and Non-Voters in a Wisconsin Primary," *Journal of Politics* 28 (1966): 589–616.

39. Paul Abramson, John Aldrich, and David Rohde, *Change and Continuity in the 1984 Elections* (Washington, D.C.: CQ Press, 1986), 121, table 4-5. The domestic-policy issues were level of government spending, government aid for minorities, government aid for women, and government support for guaranteed jobs.

40. Paul R. Abramson, John H. Aldrich, and David W. Rohde, *Change and Continuity in the 1988 Elections* (Washington, D.C.: CQ Press, 1990), 109.

41. Paul Kleppner, *Who Voted?* (New York: Praeger, 1982), 161–162.

42. Harold W. Stanley, *Voter Mobilization and the Politics of Race* (New York: Praeger, 1987), 6.
43. U.S. Department of Commerce, Bureau of the Census, *Voting and Registration in the Election of November 1986,* Current Population Reports, Series P-20, no. 414 (September 1987), 1, table A.
44. James W. Button, *Blacks and Social Change* (Princeton: Princeton University Press, 1989).
45. Ibid., 207.
46. Ibid., 213–218.
47. Earl Black and Merle Black, *Politics and Society in the South* (Cambridge: Harvard University Press, 1987), 193.

Index

Index